POLAND ADIEU

ADIEU

From Privilege to Peril

Bogdan
Broniewski

Translated from the French by Corinne Madelmont and Constance Haddad.

Edited by Constance Haddad

iUniverse, Inc.
New York   Bloomington

Poland Adieu
From Privilege to Peril

iUniverse books may be ordered through booksellers or by contacting:

iUniverse
1663 Liberty Drive
Bloomington, IN 47403
www.iuniverse.com
1-800-Authors (1-800-288-4677)

Because of the dynamic nature of the Internet, any Web addresses or links contained in this book may have changed since publication and may no longer be valid. The views expressed in this work are solely those of the author and do not necessarily reflect the views of the publisher, and the publisher hereby disclaims any responsibility for them.

ISBN: 978-1-4502-4722-1 (sc)
ISBN: 978-1-4502-4720-7 (dj)
ISBN: 978-1-4502-4721-4 (ebook)

Printed in the United States of America

iUniverse rev. date: 09/20/2010

The Family of Bogdan Broniewski

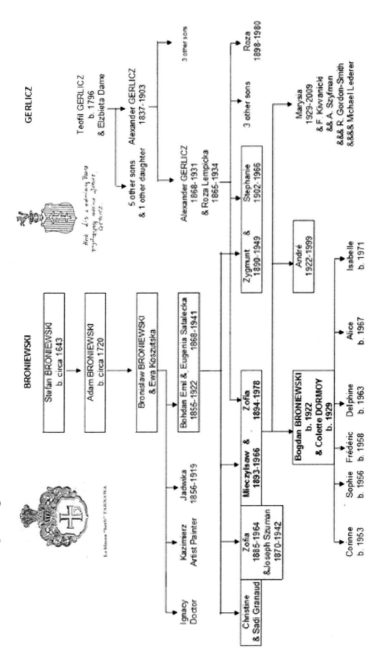

Acknowledgements

I wish to express my deepest gratitude to Colette, my wife and devoted companion of almost sixty years, for her patient assistance in correcting my grammar and spelling as I penned the first drafts of my memoirs in French.

Although French replaced my native Polish as my spoken language while I was still a teenager, I never fully addressed my childhood inattention to the finer points of the written language.

I am also deeply grateful to my daughter, Corinne Madelmont, and her friend Constance Haddad for the immeasurable hours they spent translating my work from the French into English.

Finally, my profound thanks to Constance Haddad for her careful editing and reworking of the first rough translation of three sometimes overlapping memoirs into a coherent whole.

Bogdan Broniewski

Contents

Book One: *Privilege*

Book Two: *Peril*

Preface

It was a chance encounter that led to the translation and editing of Bogdan Broniewski's memoirs. Bogdan had entrusted his oldest child, Corinne Madelmont, with translating his three separate memoirs into English: "A Spoiled Child, but Not Always Happy" (*Un Enfant Gaté*); "Exodus" (*Exode*); "In the Wake of the Marshall Plan" (*Dans le Sillage du Plan Marshall*).

Corinne, with whom I had only a casual acquaintance, asked me if I could help her with the translation of her father's work. Neither one of us was enough at home in the other's language to do the job alone, although her mastery of English far exceeded my mastery of French.

Meeting one night a week, with occasional interruptions of our schedule, we spent five years or more just putting the French into understandable English. Woven through and beyond those years were immeasurable hours spent editing the first rough translation.

During that time, although Bogdan and I never met, I came to know something of the man who wrote this memoir. As I worked and reworked the arrangement and order of words and sentences, sticking as closely as a translator and editor can to the literal translation, I marveled at how Bogdan weathered and prevailed over the extremes of both privilege and peril. In the end, the course of every life has many secrets. I leave it to others to wonder, as I did, what hidden currents shaped the character and determined the trajectory of the remarkable life that plays out in the pages of this memoir.

—Constance Haddad

Introduction

I put in writing these memories to tell the reader: this is who I am, this is where I come from, and these are the roles I have played. And for those readers who are connected by blood, this too is your history.

It begins in Poland, where I spent my first seventeen years, in a now-vanished way of life among the aristocracy of an almost feudal society. I was cosseted and indulged with all the unquestioned privileges of wealth. I was surrounded with great beauty and refinement and experienced many of the joys of a carefree boyhood. It was a life of high adventure and variety. Yet luxury and over-protection did not keep out the less joyous currents of human experience that flow through everyone's lives—jealousy, disappointment, unfulfilled longings—nor did they protect me from calamities, illness, and death. These, too, were part of the rarefied world I inhabited.

When circumstances abruptly and profoundly altered my life, with the advent of World War II, I exchanged comfort and security for hardship and danger. The family fortune was gone, and I was separated from my birthplace, my culture, and my country. I became a refugee, seeking shelter from war's turbulence. Almost immediately, I was faced with the reality that I must prepare myself, in the midst of war's chaos, to make my way in the world, based solely on my own merit and achievements. It was a difficult and sometimes treacherous journey.

The years since my youth have layered one upon another and obscured from view the person who lived through those events. Sadly, there is no one left who lived through those times with me. To know someone only after he has learned his adult role is to miss a large and profoundly revealing piece of who that person is. But I tell this story not only to say, "Remember me. I once passed this way, and this is who I was," but also because I harbor the conceit that my tale is worth telling—that my upbringing in the insular world of the Polish aristocracy, followed by a sudden and abrupt descent into the maelstrom of a war that was one of the great epics of the twentieth century, is a unique story worth the telling.

Bogdan Broniewski
Berre les Alpes, France—2009

Book One

Privilege

Chapter 1

Complacence

BEGINNINGS ARE OFTEN ANTICIPATED and celebrated. Endings often slip past us unnoticed. Only when we look back over our lives do we know when something ended: the last time we spoke to or touched someone we cared about, the last time we played a childhood game, the last time we were someplace we would never see again. Such an ending, completely beyond my imagining, abruptly altered the course of my life when I was just seventeen years old.

It was the opening of the hunting season. My brother, André, and I were planning to hunt partridges that morning. We were on the family estate, Przybyslawice, at Garbow[1] in Poland. We had wakened early, eager to be out at first light. André was just eleven months younger than I, and the two of us spent almost all of our time hunting and horseback riding. We didn't know that there was anything remarkable about our lives. Hunting and horseback riding were a centuries-old tradition among the wealthy classes in Poland. Until that day, it was the only life we had known.

The family coachman, as always, brought a horse-drawn carriage (called a *bryczka*) to our front steps. Built low to the ground, the carriage was practical for traversing difficult terrain. The coachman sat

---

1 One hundred twenty kilometers southeast of Warsaw and twenty kilometers northwest of Lublin

in front, and André and I sat in the rear, accompanied by one of our faithful dogs, Pufik, who was an eager participant in such outings.

As we rode past large ponds that surrounded the estate, we could see and hear that they were alive with the bustle and chatter of water birds. The neighboring fields were home to partridges and pheasant, and beyond lay forests that sheltered large game, including deer and wild boar. As young children, we had hunted with shotguns that could not shoot far or do much damage. Now that we were older, we owned real hunting rifles of high performance, and we expected to bring home a game bag full of partridges.

Events did not go as expected that day. We were interrupted by a distant roaring that grew louder and louder, until soon we felt the ground reverberating beneath our feet. We looked up and saw a dozen or more planes flying low overhead. It was an astonishing sight. One rarely saw planes in Poland's skies. Air travel was a thing of the future, and Poland's defense was still based almost entirely upon its cavalry, as in World War I. Our country had virtually no modern armored divisions or warplanes. Our coachman, who fancied himself an outstanding mechanic, declared confidently, "Those planes have good motors. They can't be ours. They must be German."

It was September 1, 1939. Standing in that heretofore quiet field, we were witnessing the opening hours of a war that would wreak devastation across three continents and leave between fifty million and seventy million people dead—more deaths, and in a shorter amount of time, than any other war.

André and I had lived almost obliviously to the threat of that war, although it had been hovering over Poland for more than a year. Indeed, the threat had begun earlier than that when Hitler violated the Treaty of Versailles. Under that treaty at the conclusion of World War I, the victorious powers—primarily France, Great Britain, and the United States—stipulated that the Rhineland was to remain a demilitarized zone. This region, which included the Ruhr Valley, was where heavy industry was situated and was fundamental to any German war effort. In 1936, Germany invaded the Rhineland. France and Great Britain protested vigorously, but in order to avoid an armed conflict, they let it pass.

In March 1938, the Nazis annexed Austria and, after a short while, seized part of Czechoslovakia, an area on the western border known as

Sudetenland. Soon after these alarming developments, Great Britain's Prime Minister, Neville Chamberlain, and France's Premier, Edouard Daladier, went to Munich to meet with Hitler. There was a strong sentiment to avoid war at almost any cost, particularly among the French, who had suffered the greatest losses during the deadly war years of 1914–1918.

France and Great Britain agreed to recognize Hitler's *fait accompli* in the Rhineland—as well as in Czechoslovakia and Austria. In return, Hitler was not to undertake any new military operations in Europe. All the world's newspapers showed what was to become an infamous photo of Chamberlain in his triumphant return from Munich, as he held aloft a document for a cheering crowd saying, "I bring peace in our time."

In the spring of 1938, the Wehrmacht[2] invaded the rest of Czechoslovakia. Finally, Great Britain and France understood that Hitler intended to conquer Europe. Poland would be next. Hitler was visibly searching for a pretext. German propaganda followed a previous scenario—accusations of so-called atrocities committed in Poland against German nationals. Then, the situation in Gdansk (also known by its German name, Danzig) gave Hitler another opportunity. The Treaty of Versailles stipulated that Danzig was to be a free city, managed jointly by Poland and Germany—it was situated on the Baltic Sea between the two countries. Hitler wished to annex the territory to the Reich, a demand that Poland rejected. It was clear that Hitler planned to attack, but first he sent his Minister of Foreign Affairs, Joachim von Ribbentrop, on a famous visit to Moscow, where a nonaggression pact was signed. In reality, it was a secret agreement to partition Poland between Germany and the Soviet Union along precise lines of demarcation. The agreement was signed in August 1939, less than a month before Poland was attacked. By the end of 1939, Germany and the Soviet Union would divide Poland between themselves. Again, as in the eighteenth and nineteenth centuries, Poland would be partitioned among foreign powers.

My father considered the possible dangers as he learned of German aggression and the beginning of the persecution of the Jews. Our rich Jewish friends, the Falters and Kronenbergs, were preoccupied by the situation in Germany and were considering expatriation. Perhaps this

---

2   The large German armed forces of 106 combat divisions, motorized vehicles, powerful tanks, heavy artillery, and 12,000 military aircraft

influenced my father's interest in emigrating to the United States, where he felt he would have the resources and opportunities to build an industrial fortune. But our mother was opposed to going—she did not want to be so far from her family, particularly her sisters, with whom she was very close. So the idea was abandoned. It was 1936.

Two years later, after the annexation of Czechoslovakia, German propaganda was unleashed against Poland; the meaning was clear. But my father encountered a famous clairvoyant named Ossowiecki, who, among other bits of flim-flammery, insisted that he could see a glow of light escaping a person's head, just before that person's death. Once at a reception, he had pointed to one of the guests and said, "That person is going to die in a few hours." Supposedly, his prediction proved to be true, and when the word spread, the most important people in the country wanted to consult with him. When my father met him, Ossowiecki said, "I can give you my full assurance. The war will not take place." My father apparently took this as truth, and thus our last opportunity to escape with some of our fortune in hand was lost.

Preparation for war was felt in Warsaw, where we were living during the school year, although we didn't take it very seriously. Everyone assumed that if Hitler dared to attack, the Polish army would inflict a quick and bloody defeat. André and I attended classes once a week and went on field trips, wearing military-style uniforms, several times a year, where we acted out mock attacks.

In this period, the army was regarded as an especially honorable career. We would pass soldiers in the street who wore beautifully polished boots and sparkling uniforms emblazoned with numerous decorations. When two military men passed each other, they exchanged impressive salutes. At age seventeen, I found this quite glamorous. I hung large pictures in my room that depicted the uniforms of the different military ranks. I even put up pictures of the many medals and decorations, and I developed a lifelong interest in military strategy. When a lieutenant directing our field trip exercises told me I would make a good soldier, I imagined myself as a great general. I did not, however, imagine the reality of war that we would soon face.

My youthful ignorance and indifference to world events at that time almost matched the indifference of our elders. We spent part of the summer of 1939 at Jurata, a beautiful holiday resort situated on the Hel Peninsula, which separates the Bay of Gdansk from the Baltic

Sea. Much of the elite of Polish society were vacationing at Jurata that summer. It was a very prestigious vacation spot with a deluxe hotel and individual villas that were surrounded by gardens. Our parents had built a villa there several years before and named it *Zosi*, after my mother. In the summer of 1939, the sporting events and parties were going full speed, as if that way of life would go on forever. The brilliant society of Jurata seemed unaware that in only weeks, its insular and privileged life would crash to an end.

Chapter 2

Chaos

S ANDRÉ AND I stood in the field that morning, watching the German airplanes overhead, all thoughts of hunting vanished. The world beyond our narrow, privileged lives burst through the thin veneer of comfort and security that sheltered us from uncomfortable truths, and it demanded that we instantly think and act as serious players in a life-or-death drama. Our immediate decision was to head homeward as quickly as possible. As our little coach bounced and jolted its way over the rough terrain, we sat silently, too disturbed to even talk.

It was still early in the morning when we arrived home. Just as we approached our front steps, a plane, which we recognized as one of our own, flew above us, almost touching the treetops. A few seconds later, a second plane followed at a higher altitude. Then we heard a crash in the distant fields. The German goal had been to destroy the small Polish air force on the ground. A few planes, like the one we saw, managed to fly away but were soon shot down by the superior German planes.

News of the invasion had already reached Garbow. But beyond that, the radio gave no useful information. During the hours that followed and throughout the next day, our house filled with relatives and friends who were fleeing eastward. A type of group psychosis, bordering on panic, took hold. There was enormous confusion about what to do.

My mother tried to remain calm, but her anxiety showed in every gesture and every word. She rushed to embrace André and me when we arrived home, and her voice choked as she used our pet names—André was called Jedrek, and I was known as Danek. She kept repeating, "Your father should be returning home soon."

My father was still in Warsaw on business. Phoning was extremely difficult for the phone system, which was inadequate at best, was ill-prepared to meet the demands of an emergency. Finally, late in the day, he reached us. In his short and hurried message, he said only that he was "preoccupied with events on the front" and was making "certain arrangements." The next day, early in the afternoon of September 2, he arrived home. His presence did not provide the hoped-for calming reassurance. Instead, he appeared extremely depressed and anxious. "The Germans are approaching Warsaw. The suburbs of the capital and the fortress of Modlin have been bombarded. We have to act quickly." He knew little of what was taking place elsewhere.

We later learned that early on the morning of September 1, several armored divisions had struck at strategic points throughout Poland. Supported by intense bombardment, most of the enemy divisions had penetrated deep into Polish territory. By the time the sun set that evening, Poland's fate had been sealed. And the Polish army? It had been overpowered. Its methods were pathetically outdated compared to those of the invaders—our light armaments and brave cavalry achieved some initial, brief successes, but they were soon overcome by the superior German tanks, armored cars, and air force. The Luftwaffe—the German air force—was relentlessly bombing strategic objectives throughout Poland. It struck a devastating blow at communication lines, creating widespread chaos.

The German plan consisted of two priorities: to immediately neutralize Warsaw, the center of decisions and communications; and to spare Poland's coal mines and industries in Silesia from destruction, as these were important to the future operations of the German army. This plan was perfectly executed, using a strategy devised by the famous Prussian strategist of the nineteenth century, Helmuth von Moltke. It called for a concentrated and powerful attack at one point to rupture the enemy front, and then to perform enveloping maneuvers through the breach, which would allow the attackers to encircle enemy forces and attack from the rear. This gradually created a vise-like hold upon the Polish forces, strangling and destroying them.

Poland's forces were spread too thin along the entire length of the Polish-German border, and it was soon breached. The armored units of the famous General Guderian severed the defense lines in the north, and his tanks rushed toward Warsaw and the huge fortress of Modlin. By the third day of the war, German forces reached Warsaw and, shortly thereafter, encircled it.

One should not believe, however, that there were no major battles. The Polish engaged in a fierce struggle to defend their country. But at such a price! In spite of its inferiority, the Polish military managed a desperate and courageous struggle. Acts of heroism were widespread. One example, which also illustrates Nazi methods, occurred in northern Poland. The action took place close to the mouth of the Vistula River, where it flowed into the Baltic Sea. A fort at that point, the Westerplatte, allowed a Polish garrison to control boat traffic entering the Vistula. Thus, this was an important strategic point, and the Germans considered its destruction a major priority. Shortly prior to September 1, the pre-dreadnought German battleship, the *Schleswig-Holstein*,[3] had asked permission of the garrison to pay a friendly visit. In spite of the strained political situation, the officers of Westerplatte felt it would be discourteous to refuse. At the end of August, as agreed, the battleship entered the Vistula and anchored, facing as close as possible to the fortress. While the captain of the *Schleswig-Holstein* was celebrating Polish-German friendship, his crew had important tasks to accomplish—to site, with precision, the positions of the batteries of the fortress; to locate the weak points; and especially, to adjust its twenty main artillery guns.

At four o'clock in the morning on September 1—before sunrise— the *Schleswig-Holstein* entered the mouth of the Vistula for the second time. It positioned itself at exactly the same place it had occupied before. Once this maneuver was accomplished, the ship immediately opened fire on the fortress at point-blank range with its 280 mm and 150 mm guns. The salvos lasted exactly six minutes, after which a German detachment disembarked from their ship and tried to enter the fortress through openings created by the bombardment. The Poles—armed with just three artillery pieces, four eighty-one medium mortar Stokes,

---

3   Schleswig-Holstein is a German province situated between the North Sea and the Baltic.

and forty-one machine guns—were able to repel the attack, with severe losses for the Germans. The Polish side lost four men, whereas eighty-two Germans were killed. The struggle lasted until late in the day, when the Luftwaffe joined in the battle.[4] A rain of incendiary bombs poured down on the Westerplatte. However, in spite of enormous damage, in what seemed a miracle, the Westerplatte, manned by just 182 soldiers, was able to hold out for eight days. During that time, the enemy forces of approximately 2,800 German soldiers and 800 navy men were temporarily immobilized and suffered severe losses. But on the eighth day, everything stopped. The fortress had been reduced to a mass of rocks. The Germans killed the radio telephone operator who refused to give them the radio codes, then took the approximately 113 Polish survivors into captivity. After giving military honors, they occupied the moon-like terrain—all that remained of the fortress. The Westerplatte Resistance is remembered as one of the many heroic acts of the Second World War.

The same day, not far from the desperate struggle at the fortress, another drama took place. Close to the mouth of the Vistula was a very long bridge that linked Poland to what was then known as East Prussia.[5] The bridge was of major strategic importance as a communication link for the Germans, because it was assuring the traffic between East Prussia and Poland. The destruction of the bridge would be a priority in case of conflict. The Polish army had placed mines that were ready to explode in case of attack. Again, the Germans adopted a ruse to pursue their military objective. They obtained authorization for a postal train from Prussia to cross the bridge. Before dawn on September 1, the first mail car began crossing the bridge; unlit cars, full of soldiers, followed it. At the rear of the train was an armored convoy loaded with heavy artillery. When the postal train was barely onto the bridge, the German detachments, not unaware of the possibility that the Poles might have suspected their real intent, rushed toward the pylons in order to cut the lines that linked to the detonators. The valiant Polish sentinels who were guarding the bridge immediately responded. As the German

---

4   The Luftwaffe used forty Junkers Ju 87 Stuka dive bombers and seven other aircraft, including the Heinkel He 51, Junkers Ju 52, and the most well-known of all the German aircraft, the Messerschmitt. It later turned out that these formidable aircraft were outperformed by the British Spitfires and Hurricanes—a decisive factor in the Battle of Britain.

5   East Prussia was the result of a partitioning of Poland in the late 1700s. After World War II, this area was returned to Poland.

troops on the bridge were swept with machine gun fire, a spectacular scene erupted. The Poles activated the detonators, causing the entire bridge to collapse. The train and all its cargo, including clusters of German soldiers and armored cars, catapulted from the bridge into the waters of the Vistula. The river was a chaotic scene of the dead and near-dead in a river choked with tons of wreckage.

From the second day of the German offensive, Warsaw was in danger. The Polish troops at the central front received orders to withdraw toward Warsaw in order to defend it; they never arrived. As the Polish armies were pulling back from the Poznan region toward Warsaw, the Germans were converging toward them from every direction. Caught in a vise, attacked from the north and south, the Polish divisions were cut into smaller and smaller pieces by Wehrmacht tanks until they were wiped out. The clashes went on for eight days; later, there were reports of numerous acts of heroism in this desperate struggle.

As the defense reached its end, the commander, General Wiad, who had been grievously wounded in combat that day, addressed his surviving troops: "We have tried hard until the end to break through. I can do nothing more to help Warsaw. My place is to repose here with my dead soldiers." He died two hours later. Before dying, he dictated to the chaplain several words for his wife: "I die for the country; make our son a brave Pole; I have confessed."

Ignorant of all these dramas that were playing out, our family and the cluster of relatives and friends we were sheltering engaged in intense, emotionally wrenching discussions of what to do. On the third day of September, my aunt and uncle, Stefanie and Zygmunt, arrived. They were carrying rumors and bits of news they had picked up as they hurried to join the family. A decisive meeting was held with our parents. Zygmunt argued forcefully, "You have two sons almost old enough to serve in the military. You have to get them away from the Nazis." He and Stefanie believed that they could stay and take care of our estate at Garbow. This proved to be a brave but tragic decision, particularly for our beloved Aunt Stefanie.

It had not occurred to us, only two days before, when we saw the German planes overhead and put our guns aside to hurry back home, that our lives were about to change forever. We were totally unprepared to depart and leave everything behind—all of our belongings and, most heart-breaking of all, the people we loved, particularly Zygmunt and Stefanie. This scenario had never entered anyone's mind. In any case, there was little time for reflection. News was filtering in that German troops were progressing on a broad front in Poland. Warsaw could be reached in a matter of days. We had to make rapid decisions. It appeared that the only—or safest—option was to head for the Romanian border.

This decision was briefly reconsidered, throwing us again into chaos, when the radio announced that France and Great Britain, honoring the treaty signed only weeks earlier with Poland, had declared war on Nazi Germany. Our hopes were temporarily raised. Perhaps the Allies would aid Poland, or perhaps they would attack Germany. But these hopes quickly evaporated before the realities on the ground. Unfortunately, none of the three countries—France, Great Britain, Poland—was prepared for war; we had all focused more on defense. France had been counting on its Maginot Line, a thick concrete fortification that was constructed along its borders with Germany and Italy and was considered an impenetrable barrier against any powerful aggressor. Great Britain, with the most powerful navy in the world, felt protected against a German invasion. Poland based its defense almost entirely on its cavalry, as it had done for centuries. None of the three countries—but particularly Poland—had modern armored divisions or warplanes in the quantity and quality necessary to measure up against the Germans.

On the evening of September 3, the decision was made to leave for Zaleszczyki, a Polish town situated on the Romanian border. We devoted the next two days to preparations for our departure. At the last moment before leaving Warsaw, my father withdrew everything held in the safe-deposit at the bank. This included jewels, gold coins, and cash. My mother, helped by a maid, was sewing little sacks to contain jewels and money. André and I, and our sister, Marysia, were to hang the sacks around our necks and conceal them beneath our clothes. As we tried to figure out which few possessions we could take, I asked about taking our guns. My father quickly responded, "You won't be needing them." The uncompromising tone of his words struck me more than anything that had been said to that point. It wasn't the loss of the guns—it was what they signified: we were being abruptly cut loose from everything we knew and seized by events that we could neither understand nor control. It was like a sudden, unexpected death—an ending that strikes with the force of a physical blow; and, as with death, there was nothing to be negotiated—no concessions, no more time. We had to pick ourselves up, regain our breath, and move on.

Like millions of other people who would be swept up in the tempests of war, our lives were being ripped from their moorings. Nothing had prepared us for the cataclysmic changes we were about to face. It would be a long and sometimes treacherous journey in search of a safe harbor. When at last we could look back over the miles and years that separated us from the world we left behind, we would see that the way of life we had known, rooted in aristocratic traditions of earlier centuries, was gone forever.

Chapter 3

Garbow—The Beginning

FROM BIRTH, I HAD known all the protection from hardship that money could provide. I was born on February 2, 1922, in the beloved family home, Przybyslawice, which was part of the Garbow domain, a vast estate of two thousand hectares. I was named Bogdan, a slight variation upon my grandfather's name, Bohdan. My brother, André, was born eleven months later. We were pampered and catered to by nannies, governesses, and tutors. Josephine, a middle-aged woman, was dedicated entirely to my care, and Francoise, who had been my mother's chambermaid and was very devoted to our family, took care of André. We were like sons to them. They adored us, and rivalries developed between them as each pretended that her charge was the more clever.

Our home was a typical manor house for landed estates of that time and place. Greek style columns ornamented the entry and, although only a single story, the dwelling was quite large and exquisitely furnished. The chandelier in the dining room was so heavy that the ceiling had to be reinforced to hold its weight. It was a spectacular sight when all of its three hundred candles were lit.

Our home's opulent appearance, however, belied its lack of amenities. Electricity had not spread to that part of the world when I was young, nor had running water or central heating. Lighting depended principally upon gaslights, and water came from a deep well dug not far from the house. But we did not feel the lack of what we had never known, and we had servants to shield us from all possible inconveniences.

Water in the house came from a tank in the attic that had to be filled each day by two strong men operating a pump at the well. Our heat came from coal stoves in every room, which servants kept stoked all day long. Our bread was baked in a large kitchen equipped with a huge oven, where enough bread could be baked in one day to last all week. Our linens, and even some of our clothes, were sewn on a pedal-operated machine in a large room reserved just for sewing. Our perishable food was kept in a deep cave that had been dug on a neighboring manor. This was our icebox, thanks to the reserves of ice deposited in the winter. Most of our vegetables and fruit were grown on approximately one-half of the ten hectares of gardens that surrounded our residence.

The history of Garbow[6] is described in documents going back to the fourteenth century. In 1903, it had to be auctioned off to pay the creditors of its ruined heir, a descendent of the several counts Jezierski. He had managed, in less than two years, to wipe out an immense family fortune in the gambling casinos of Warsaw.

It was then that my grandfather, the diminutive Bohdan Broniewski, entered the scene. He was forty-eight years old when he arrived at the auction, accompanied by an assistant carrying a valise full of bank notes. (It's possible that the valise also held rubles, for Russian money was then in circulation in Poland.) An auction of that size was unusual, and it attracted mostly onlookers, for few had the wealth to be serious bidders. Bohdan, a good-looking man with a handlebar moustache, a short beard, and an intense expression, quickly dominated the auction. He paid everything in cash and became the owner of the Garbow domain. This was not the first such transaction for my grandfather, but it was perhaps the largest. He had accumulated great wealth through a number of such ventures.

Like his father, Bronislaw, Bohdan had graduated from the University of Vienna as a chemical engineer. He began working in

---

6   Actually, the manor was built in the nineteenth century on the site of a magnificent, early eighteenth-century palace, which had been owned by the grand aristocratic family of the princes Czartoryski, who controlled enormous stretches of land in Poland until, as punishment for insubordination, their lands were confiscated by the Russian czar Nicholas I. The palace was burned down, and later the Jezierskis built the manor that we occupied.

a sugar refinery and soon took over its management. In a few years, he'd enlarged the operation to extend well beyond the sugar business. Everything he touched, he improved and expanded, whether it was in agriculture or business or finance.

By the time of his death, he had expanded Garbow well beyond purely agricultural concerns. There was a brick factory, a sugar refinery, a beer distillery, a vodka distillery, a horse-breeding enterprise, a timber industry, and a fish-farming enterprise. The latter was a successful venture started in the nineteenth century by its former owners, the Jezierski counts.

Almost everything that was needed for the various enterprises was grown or produced at Garbow: all the hops for beer-making, all the sugar beets, all the grain for the horses, and all the potatoes and grain for the vodka distillery. Bricks from the brick factory were used to build a several-stories-high building for drying hops, as well as a sugar refinery. All the wood needed for construction came from the Garbow forests. Although there were numerous large domains in Poland, Garbow, by its level of industrialization, occupied a unique place, and my grandfather Bohdan became one of the pillars of Polish industry for that period. Indeed, he became the Minister of Industry and contributed to the development of the railroads at the beginning of the twentieth century.

Unlike so many of the rich and powerful, who often were ruthless and insensitive to the point of inhumanity, Bohdan was known for his generosity and good heart. His memory lived long after his death at age sixty-seven, particularly among people of modest means, whom he had helped when they were in need, sometimes rescuing them from desperate situations. He even built an enormous church at Garbow, a veritable cathedral, with bricks he donated.

I was told that at my birth, he sat contemplating my cradle, happy to see that the succession of the Broniewski family was assured. Sadly, I never knew him, for he died when I was eight months old. Perhaps it was fortunate that he didn't live to see the tumultuous and sometimes tragic lives of his children.

Chapter 4

Bohdan's Heirs

M Y FATHER, MIECZYSLAW, WAS one of four children born to Bohdan and my grandmother Eugenie, an exceptionally beautiful woman from a wealthy Viennese family. Their first child, a daughter, was named Zofia. Then came Zygmunt and next, my father. When Eugenie was forty-two years old, she gave birth to their fourth and last child, Christine, who was twelve to twenty years younger than her siblings.

Zygmunt was born in 1890, and my father in 1893. It was their father's intention, from their earliest years, that Zygmunt, his eldest son, would become the administrator of the Garbow domain. Fate was to interrupt that twice, the last time with tragic finality.

When Zygmunt graduated from the Academie Agricole de Hohenheim in Stuttgart, Germany, he was required to go into military service. Poland at that time was under the occupation of three different powers: Germany, Austria, and czarist Russia.[7] Thus, Zygmunt had to serve in the Russian army. He was in the army when the war of 1914–1918 broke out, but when the Bolshevik Revolution of 1916 changed the balance of powers in Europe, the czarist army was disbanded, and Zygmunt returned to Poland.

Near the end of the war, he enlisted in the army that was just

---

7   Poor Poland was invaded, conquered, occupied, and divided so many times that it is no wonder that its national anthem is "Poland Has Not Yet Perished."

forming under the leadership of the great Polish hero Jozef Pilsudski. He helped defend his country against the invasion of the Red Cavalry army, which was under the command of the renowned Marshal Budenny. Zygmunt distinguished himself in the victorious battle of 1919 that repulsed the Soviets back to their national borders. He was decorated with the highest Polish military distinction, *Virtuti Militari,* and promoted to the rank of major.

Demobilized at the end of the hostilities in 1919, my uncle then was able to devote himself to the administration of Garbow. If one didn't know his whole life story, it would be easy to assume that agriculture was the only pursuit of this quiet man. I remember him very well; moving about tirelessly in a horse-drawn carriage. He was everywhere, watching over all the agricultural and industrial activities. As soon as I was old enough, he would sometimes let me sit beside him, and he would patiently explain the intriguing operations he was overseeing. Wherever Zygmunt went, he was always accompanied by a little cocker spaniel named Kulka ("little ball"). The faithfulness of this dog was legendary. I think she died of a broken heart when war again took Zygmunt away from Garbow.

My father, Mieczyslaw, like his father, Bohdan, earned a degree in chemical engineering. He graduated from Gratz Polytechnique in Vienna at the end of World War I and went to work as an assistant to his father. When Bohdan died four years later, my father and Zygmunt each inherited half of their father's estate. Zygmunt was in charge of administering Garbow, and my father was entirely involved with the sugar production and other expanding business interests in his father's wide ranging industrial empire. At least outwardly, it appeared to be a wise division of responsibilities.

Zygmunt moved and spoke with the commanding presence of a man used to giving orders, and he held himself with the erect bearing that hinted at his military background. Although reserved, he was fair and kind in his dealings with his workers, and he seemed to thrive on handling the complex operations at Garbow. A photo of him shows a good-looking man with his hair parted in the middle and plastered tightly to his head. He had a pleasant gaze beneath a square brow and a neat little mustache over a full mouth. His photo revealed less of the man, however, than did his brother's photos.

My father, a dark-haired, dark-eyed man of medium height and strong build, was a more outgoing person than Zygmunt. He radiated the bonhomie of a man at ease with his own importance, one who relished both the challenges of the business world and the social life enjoyed by the wealthy and socially prominent. Photos always showed him looking straight at the camera with a confident smile and the strong, forceful gaze of a successful man.

He and Zygmunt were married to sisters; thus, the families were very close. My father was married to Zofia, the older of the two sisters and the more sedate and conventional of the two. Like her husband, she was of a sturdy—though softer—frame, but she was fair-skinned and blue-eyed. Unlike her husband, whose wealth dated back only one generation, my mother came from a long history of wealth. She wore her social position with the unquestioning manner of someone who had never known anything else, but she wore it without ostentation. She was a loving and devoted mother and although unburdened by the tedium of household chores, she was kept busy with overseeing servants and workers in a large and complex household. She did this in an even-tempered and good-natured manner, seeming comfortable as she moved back and forth between the domestic world and the sparkling social milieu upon which my father thrived.

Zygmunt was married to our remarkable Aunt Stefanie, who was a sportswoman and hunter without equal. Stefanie was responsible for much of André's and my prowess at riding and hunting. She was our instructor, our good friend, and often, our confidant. Unlike her softly curved sister, she had a lithe and athletic frame. She had no children of her own and was young and energetic in spirit. She participated with her husband in the management of Garbow with great enthusiasm, as was her habit with everything else she undertook. Horses were her special field. She was the one who actually started raising horses for the Polish army. It was an agreeable and lucrative activity at that time, for horses had been a vital part of Polish life for centuries. Unfortunately, their essential role in transportation and warfare was waning, but few people recognized that the days of cavalry warfare were about to end.

Stefanie's photos show a lovely face that could only hint at her strong and brilliant personality. Any compromise with conventional beauty only served to emphasize the force of her character. She was as good or better a rider and hunter than any man. She was quick to laugh, loved to joke, and was more an adventurous, fun-loving companion than the dignified aunt one might have expected. Once, she confided to our mother that if she and Zygmunt had been living on a deserted island, and Zygmunt had been the only man on that island, she would not have married him. However, except for the fact that they could not have children, they seemed to be a happy couple. They did have one trait in common that became clear later, under dramatic and tragic circumstances—it was their great courage, no matter what the adversity or how extreme the danger.

Another aunt, Christine, who was our father's and Zygmunt's much-younger sister, led a life that took a number of dramatic twists and turns. Although she played a much smaller role in my life than Zygmunt and Stefanie, that small role made a deep impression on me.

Her strange journey began when, as a very young woman, she was seduced by a handsome and unscrupulous man with whom she had fallen in love. Unfortunately, it turned out that this handsome man was already married. As was common in such situations at that time and place, it seemed to Christine that there was only one course of action open for her—she must go into a convent. Nothing was able to shake her conviction, including the arguments of her older brother, my father. He couldn't see his vivacious, rather headstrong little sister spending the rest of her life in a convent, particularly because it was not a vocation but more of a desperate action as the result of a tragic love affair.

I was seven or eight years old when this occurred, and I found it very disturbing. We attended a ceremony in the cloister of the Carmelites at Poznan, an important town in western Poland. In making her eternal vows, Christine committed herself to accepting the very severe rules of the Carmelites. She was to be forever cut off from any contact with family members and to separate herself from all worldly goods, which included ceding to the convent her very sizeable inheritance from her father, Bohdan. She entered the convent as an apprentice sister and took her vows two years later. This waiting period was to give her time to reflect and act in full knowledge of the irreversible decision she would be making.

After a long farewell mass, everyone cried. The gates closed, separating Christine forever from her mother and family. I spoke to her for the last time through a barred window. It was as if she were being taken away to the gallows. I was very troubled. My mother tried to reassure me by explaining that Christine was now going to give her life to Christ and pray for my eternal salvation. I didn't find that comforting.

No one could have foreseen, however, the eventful existence that lay ahead for Christine. She had a very strong personality, and it turned out that she was ill-suited to spending the rest of her life in meditation and prayer. What to do? She had made her eternal vows. After many difficulties and with the authorization of the Vatican, a solution was found. Christine would go to Africa as a missionary sister. This life suited her better. She was able to put her considerable energy into working as a nurse. It was assumed that she had found her calling and would spend the rest of her life ministering to the needy. But an unexpected element entered the scene in the person of a missionary father, or as was said in French, *un père blanc*. In a photo she sent the family, we saw a tall and alluring-looking man, smiling at the camera (possibly held by Christine?) with a far too warm and intimate a smile. The inevitable occurred—Christine and the *père blanc* fell in love. They abandoned the mission and left Africa together. We didn't know where she went, and we didn't hear from her for a number of years.

When she finally reappeared and made contact with her family, she was working as a nurse in a hospital in the southwest of France. She insisted that no one was to know that she had been religious in the past. By this time, she and the *père blanc* had gone their separate ways, but one of her patients in the hospital, who had been a shopkeeper, fell in love with her and asked her to marry him. The two of them acquired a modest hotel and café. It was there that my father saw his little sister again, for the first and last time, after more than twenty-five years. She was over fifty years old. After the death of her husband, Christine retired to a small village in southern France. She lived as a recluse, without contact with her relatives, until her death.

Chapter 5

The Gerlicz Family

MY MOTHER, ZOFIA GERLICZ, was born in 1894. She came from a family no less colorful than my father's, but her father, Aleksander Gerlicz, unlike my other grandfather, Bohdan, who was a self-made man, came from landed aristocracy that went back many generations.[8]

Part of my mother's youth was spent in the chateau on the Stara Wies domain.[9] She would tell stories of the luxurious existence in this princely residence. The grand salon had walls painted raspberry red and an enormous fireplace covered with antique ceramics. The hunting room was decorated with paneling made of precious woods and had a monumental stairway to the second floor. The façade was adorned with the coat of arms of successive owners, including that of the Gerlicz family: *Liz z odmiana Bzura.*[10]

My grandfather, Aleksander Gerlicz, died when I was nine years

---

8   The Gerlicz family lineage included Aleksander Junior (1868–1931); Aleksander Senior (1837–1907); Teofil, born in 1796; Kasper, born in 1756; Marcin, born in 1729; Jerzy, born in 1690; and on back through the generations.

9   It was located about 80 kilometers northeast of Warsaw. It suffered much damage during World War II but was subsequently perfectly restored by the government and now serves as a place for official receptions. The beautiful park of thirty-two hectares, with two large ponds that surrounded the chateau, was carefully restored.

10   The coats of arms, or heraldic emblems, were a certificate of nobility granted by the king as a reward for services rendered—often on the field of battle. The same coat of arms could belong to several families with different names. In other cases, families having the same name but belonging to different branches might have different coats of arms. One could

old. He was a man of severe mien that belied his good heart. Each time he and our grandmother visited us, they brought presents. An old photo shows him arriving in their large Phaeton convertible, something quite rare in Poland at that time. It was 1928 or '29. He was about sixty years old—slender, white-haired, with a perfectly trimmed goatee. He looked at the camera with a strong, serious gaze.

I remember being particularly impressed by his car. The chauffeur had to exert great effort when it was necessary to install the top to the convertible. The operation would last a half-hour or more. In those days, there was neither the material nor the technology that later made the process quite simple.

My grandfather Gerlicz moved with considerable difficulty because he had only one good leg; the other was of wood. At the turn of the century, he and a cousin had been traveling through a dark forest on their way to a neighboring town, when brigands attacked their carriage. Certain regions of Poland, at that time, were covered with forests, and the roads through them were quite dangerous. Gunfire was exchanged; the brigands scattered, but the coachman was killed, and my grandfather was wounded in the leg. My mother, who was then a child, remembered waking in the night to a scene of horror. The servants were carrying her father to a couch, where he lay weakened and bleeding. Hygienic conditions were almost nonexistent then, such that radical measures were necessary to avoid gangrene. His leg had to be amputated. The operation was performed with whatever sharp implements were at hand.

Aleksander Gerlicz's wife, born Rosa Lempicka, also came from a family of great landed wealth. She was the daughter of Konstantin Lempicka. The family name of Lempicka was found only in this part of Poland. It is possible that the owner of a house of high fashion in Paris, Lolita Lempicka, descended from Konstantin.

Like all families, if one looks back through several generations, an interesting mix of forbears will show up—some that add luster to the family tree, some who are quite ordinary, and others who are an embarrassment—or worse. Among the distinguished ancestors was my great-grandfather, the senior Aleksander, who was married to Konstancja Finke de Finkenthal. My mother remembered her well, as

---

identify a noble family by the usage of a specific name and coat of arms. Most of the meaning of this coat of arms is buried in history.

she was widely known for her social and cultural activities. She was the great-granddaughter of Benjamin Finke, who was born in 1741 to a Swiss immigrant who emigrated to Poland at the behest of King August II. Although only a miller by trade, Benjamin Finke played an important role in Polish history. He became a financier and businessman and was active in the political world of the eighteenth century. He once gave refuge to the last king of Poland, Stanislaw Poniatowski, and was made a noble by Emperor Francois II of Austria.

Another eminence on the Gerlicz family tree was Aleksander Senior's grandson, who became the archbishop of France, Cardinal Piotr Maria Gerlier (1882–1967). Although he changed the spelling of his name from Gerlicz to the more Franco spelling of Gerlier, he remained forever faithful to his heritage and always helped his Polish compatriots.

My mother had two sisters: Roza, who lived in Warsaw; and Stefanie, who was a dominant figure in my life. Though different in personality, all three sisters were strong, capable people. But their three brothers—tall and handsome young men—proved to be ill-begotten fruit of the family tree. Two among them married rich heiresses with dowries that included prestigious domains. The oldest, Aleksander, married Anna (Aunt Anula), a young widow full of life, who was close to my mother. The second brother, Jan, married Hanna, and the third brother, Seweryn, remained single. Marriage made Aleksander the proprietor of two large domains. He lived extravagantly, showing no restraint. After several years, he was short of money and regularly asked my father for help. His brother Jan was even worse, but before completely wiping out Hanna's large fortune, he managed to die a heroic death. While still recovering from a heart attack, he left on an urgent trip to Lublin and happened upon a village that was on fire. He rushed into a burning house and rescued an old woman, carrying her out on his shoulders. Shortly thereafter, his chauffeur found him dead in his hotel room in Lublin. Apparently, his weakened heart was not ready for such acts of heroism.

A short time later, another drama played out in that same hotel. Aunt Anula's son, after a dinner with too much to drink, went to bed while smoking a cigarette. During his sleep, the cigarette fell on his chest, and he was badly burned. The maid found him the next morning in front of the sink, trying to tend to his burns. He suffered horribly and died two days later.

My mother's youngest brother, Seweryn, visited us occasionally at Przybyslawice. On one such visit, he seemed extremely depressed. I remember seeing him in a small sitting room with my mother, where she was consoling him. I was only seven or eight years old at the time and didn't understand what was going on. Later, someone told me that Seweryn had had a tragic love affair.

Several days after his visit, he organized a little reception at his home. During the course of the evening, he retired to his apartments. A shot rang out, and his friends rushed to his room, where they found him sitting at his desk, surrounded by gun smoke. Gravely wounded, he begged his friends to save him, but he died shortly thereafter. He was only twenty-seven years old. It was a double tragedy for my grandmother—the loss of her favorite son and a suicide, which was a sin in the eyes of the Catholic Church.

Chapter 6

Change and Progress

WHEN ANDRÉ AND I were still very young, our parents undertook a huge task—to completely renovate the immense park that surrounded Przybyslawice, our home on the Garbow domain. They wanted to have a garden that would rival the prestigious gardens they had seen on their travels in foreign countries, particularly Italy—this, in spite of the fact that Poland had a colder climate with relatively short summers. They hired the most famous landscape designer in Warsaw to undertake this grandiose project, a Mr. Zycinski. He was responsible for all the parks in Warsaw and lived in a villa provided by the government in the famous Lazienki Park.

Apparently, Mr. Zycinski was given carte blanche, for he imported exotic species, such as agaves, palm, bananas, and many other plants which normally grow in warmer climates. This was an audacious gamble. It was necessary to not only import the plants from great distances but also to import the appropriate soil for each plant. Sometimes new means of transporting and handling the plants had to be developed— and all this in a country where the necessary infrastructure was sorely lacking. Also, to protect all this exotic vegetation, it was necessary to construct greenhouses. One large and several smaller structures, made almost entirely of glass, were built at the rear of the park. An elaborate system of acclimatization controlled their interior temperatures and humidity.

One area of the park resembled a botanical garden, with a large variety of rare and exceptional plants that surrounded an elaborate fountain. Huge rocks were brought in from the Carpates Mountains to add more drama to the garden. The entire project was under construction for several years and demanded enormous effort. My mother, who loved flowers and had studied gardening, became personally involved, making several trips to Holland to select different species. It was her influence that led to flower-covered arbors, trellises, and a large pergola.

For Mr. Zycinski, the creation of this park represented the crowning achievement of his career. He gave his all to it, supervising every detail of the project. Almost every week, he came to Przybyslawice to oversee a flurry of work, while surrounded by people from all the different trades. André and I would watch from afar as he barked his orders like a commanding general and delivered withering assessments of any performance that didn't meet his high standards. Workers detested him for his demanding and forceful manner.

When the garden was completed, it equaled and exceeded our parents' dreams. It was a mixture of large native trees, exquisite flowers, an impressive collection of plants suited to a Mediterranean or semi-tropical climate, and dramatic design features. Its immense size and design were spectacular. However, the exotic plants were not suitable for the Polish climate and had to stay in the greenhouses for much of the year. Moreover, having to move the plants back and forth was a fussy job, causing some damage to both the plants and the paths they traversed. And no one had thought about whether a park of such sophistication would appear out of place, not only in our climate but in relation to our house, which was of a traditional Polish style—not an Italian villa. Clearly, Mr. Zycinski and my parents were oblivious to this.

Unfortunately, Mr. Zycinski never got to enjoy his success. His health declined rapidly. I remember the last time he visited at Przybyslawice. As was his habit, he stayed to dinner. I was struck by his pallor and the change in his appearance. Over the course of the evening, we heard sinister rumblings coming from his stomach. He simply said, "My insides are revolting." He returned to Warsaw that evening, and we never saw him again. He died of cancer several months later.

For André and me, the elaborate gardens were grander than any child's fantasies—a source of unbounded joy. The dense vegetation and variety of landscape were a constant inspiration for games and imaginative play. An actual labyrinth had been created, with a vast network of hedge-lined paths. Endless hiding places could be found behind masses of greenery and under centuries-old linden, oak, and chestnut trees. Twelve dogs of different breeds, most of them long-haired dachshunds, were my constant companions as I explored every corner of the lush landscape.

While our grandiose garden—a virtual park in size and design—was certainly a major change, it could hardly be characterized as progress. Gradually, however, my father, who always was interested in making use of the very latest technical advances, began to introduce some modern conveniences at Garbow that truly did represent significant progress. His first priority was electricity.

Of the many enterprises that were part of the Garbow domain, one of the largest was the sugar refinery. An electric generator was installed that was driven by a turbine receiving steam from the refinery's furnace. Cables were extended from the generator to provide electricity for our property. This was considerable progress—the pumping of water could now be done by electricity. Unfortunately, power failures were very common. Often, at the most inappropriate times, everything would go off. We would all say, "The belt snapped," and repairs would proceed promptly, in order to avoid upsetting the boss.

Next came a real tour de force. There wasn't a telephone in the entire Garbow region, but with the will and money, amazing things could be accomplished. Unfortunately, transmission was very poor, and it was necessary to shout to be heard. This was the cause of a number of little dramas. When André's governess, Francoise, tried to communicate to our parents, who were in Warsaw, that André had a sore throat, her confusion in translating from the French *mal a la gorge* to the Polish for throat, *gardlo,* led to a mispronunciation that confused and annoyed my father, and reduced Francoise to tears,

Naturally, as soon as it was possible, my father bought a car—possible, that is, because there was a shortage of roads on which to drive a car. Gradually, however, after the First World War, the automobile played an increasing role in people's lives. My father was generally able to make his weekly trip of 120 kilometers (75 miles) between Warsaw and Przybyslawice in four hours.

For my mother, who went often to Warsaw, it was more practical to take the train. She had to use a *caleche,* a small, light, horse-drawn carriage—practical for trips of a short distance—to get from our home to a train station in a neighboring town. In contrast to the larger carriages, the less luxurious caleche was uncovered, but the passengers were protected by a moveable hood that could be raised when needed.

When I was still too young to go out riding alone, I was often allowed to accompany the caleche on horseback. Once, as the coachman was leaving to pick up my mother at the train station, I decided to follow on horseback. Just as I was about to leave, however, black clouds began to obscure the horizon. My governess forbade me to leave, but I didn't listen to her. On the return trip, a violent storm struck. My mother ordered me to get off the horse and to shelter myself beside her in the caleche, leaving the mount in the hands of the coachman. This presented the poor coachman with the task of holding the reins of my horse, while at the same time managing the caleche on a narrow and sodden road in the middle of a storm. At a curve in the road, the caleche veered off and became stuck in a field, at which time my horse broke loose and galloped home to his stable—causing great excitement for the grooms. The coachman, soaked and covered with mud, was finally able to get the caleche free. As for my role, it had been inglorious, and I was confined to the caleche and subjected to my mother's fury.

My mother's little caleche was the last of the horse-drawn vehicles to remain in use. It was housed in a vast structure with other carriages inside the *fulwark*—a walled area that also contained a stable, a barn, a storage shed, and a separate workplace for both the carpenter and the blacksmith. As soon as I was old enough to venture beyond the tall brick wall that surrounded our gardens, I found the fulwark a fascinating world to explore. It was the nerve center of all the agricultural activities at Garbow. Most of the farm equipment was made by the artisans at the fulwark. These workers, along with many other people employed at Garbow, were provided with living quarters that were part of the domain. In turn, they looked after everything within the fulwark, including the carriages.

The principal carriage was called a *kareta*. It consisted of a closed cab, attached to a chassis, with an elaborate suspension that was designed to cushion against the shocks caused by bad roads. The cab was large, well-enclosed, padded, and equipped with comfortable seats—clearly intended to provide maximum comfort on long journeys. Nevertheless, from stories told by my grandfather Gerlicz, the trips were long and arduous, particularly in winter, when the roads were covered with snow. They also could be dangerous—it was in such a carriage that my grandfather was attacked by bandits.

In examining the interior of the carriage, I found numerous objects, notably toiletries, for making long journeys more agreeable. Among these, one especially caught my attention—it was a chamber pot. I understood the usage at once but wondered what the coachman then did with it. I was told, "Oh, well, he takes care of it." I tried to imagine the miseries of the coachman, exposed to bad weather, faced with all kinds of dangers and discomforts, and then, dealing with his passengers' chamber pots.

Beside the kareta was a carriage with wheels that could be replaced by runners when deep snow made the use of wheels impossible. The two carriages were well-cared for but I never saw them in use. They became museum pieces—the arrival of trains, and later the automobile, made this inevitable.

When the first automobile finally arrived, it was housed in its own separate garage, situated elsewhere. The purpose of this separation was not only a practical one but also to assure the clear distinction between the superior stature of the chauffeur of the automobile and the coachman for the horse-drawn vehicles.

It took a long time, however, for there to be any wide usage of automobiles because of the lack of good roads. Except for the main highways, the roads were dirt and often impassable. Not far from Garbow was a principal, strategic artery that connected Warsaw to Lublin. From there it went on to Lvov and then to the Soviet frontier. It was by this route that the Polish army would have to travel, if attacked by Communist forces. The authorities devoted large resources in an attempt to make this route passable. The only method, at that time, was to use either rocks or paving stones, for asphalt was not yet available. I witnessed the preparation of these surfaces. It was a staggering spectacle—impossible to forget. Hundreds of workers, in a long line stretching along the roadway, would sit or squat on the ground as they broke rocks and cut them into paving stones. They were exposed to bad weather and wore neither protective glasses nor gloves. In Poland, this was considered the most arduous and miserable work possible. A common expression used when one wanted to refuse work was "I would rather break rocks on the road."

In spite of all the effort and sacrifice, however, the roads remained mediocre for a long time. They couldn't even hold up against the stream of cars on the very first day of the German invasion. But the automobile age, which was already well established in much of the industrialized world, was coming inexorably to the backwaters of Poland.

Chapter 7

Family Ties and Tensions

IN OUR MILIEU, THE relationship between parents and children was more formal than most. As in many families, my father was absorbed in business and did not find much time to devote to his children. We didn't even dine with our parents, as was the custom in wealthy families. Thus, there was less opportunity for our father to really know his children, and he made judgments based on superficial observations.

I don't remember when I began to be aware that he favored André. It was nothing very overt, and he certainly was a devoted parent, but good intentions cannot protect us from some realities. Perhaps André's physical resemblance to him—they were both dark, with similar features—made him think that he and André shared other qualities. From the very beginning, they had an easier relationship. It was our father's plan that André would follow in his footsteps in the business world.

I was fair, like my mother's side of the family. Early photos show me as a sturdy, plump-cheeked child, with my blond hair in a Dutch-boy haircut. I had a tendency to stutter, which gave me the appearance of being a rather nervous, emotional child, unable to express myself without some difficulty. This caused my father to see me as more suited to less complex tasks, and thus, I was to be relegated to the world of agriculture.

My mother, who understood me well and appreciated me, had a different view of things. In any case, I was her favorite. This partiality that each parent displayed toward a particular son would cause problems of many kinds—for both André and me—and would manifest in profound ways throughout our lives. From the time André and I were very young, serious outbursts of jealousy affected our relationship. Perhaps we were not that much different from many families, where competition for a parent's affection plays out in endless forms of sibling rivalry.

We lived surrounded with an over-abundance of expensive toys and possessions that were the cause of many fights. Our Gerlicz grandparents, with the best of intentions, would bring us gifts and toys every time they visited. We were completely spoiled and had no understanding and appreciation of our good fortune. Indeed, the village child, clutching a precious rag doll or pulling a wooden wagon that his or her father had made, might well have been happier than we were in our palace of plenty. In spite of the almost never-ending choices of toys, we ended up fighting for the same object, even if there were several alike.

I remember still a visit from our grandparents, who had just returned from a foreign trip. They gave André and me two beautiful Swiss watches that our mother had admired. On taking leave of our parents, our grandparents stopped in our room to give us their usual farewell hugs. A deplorable spectacle welcomed them. André and I were fighting over the watches—actually throwing them at each other. The look of shock and disappointment on my grandparents' faces lingers still in my mind.

One of our fights even left me with a lifelong scar. Each summer, our parents would have sand trucked in from a nearby lagoon to freshly fill our sandbox. We would wait impatiently for the arrival of the vehicles that would bring our new sand. For the first few days, all would be harmonious in the sandbox. One time, however, I was squatting at André's feet when an argument took place. He seized a little metal shovel and struck me with it, causing a deep cut on my head. Stitches were unknown to us at that time, and it took a long time to stop the bleeding. This resulted in much comforting from my mother and disgrace for André.

Even my happy memories of boyhood pursuits are sometimes

accompanied by memories of difficulties or suffering. Our father liked dogs and from our early years, he regularly provided us with dogs as playmates. Our first dogs were long-haired Pomeranians. They were playful, intelligent dogs, and we would become inseparable. One day tragedy struck. A rabid dog appeared at Garbow and fought with our dogs. There was no vaccine for rabies available in Poland at that time. Unable to take a chance, my father ordered all the dogs shot. We were told to stay in the house. I stood by the windows and watched one of our workers pass by carrying a hunting rifle. Soon, shots rang out. I felt as if each one pierced my heart. I was too stricken to watch. By chance, one dog was spared because he had been locked up and had no contact with the rabid animal. This one surviving dog let out pathetic, blood-curdling howls the entire time. He had to have known what was happening. Shortly later, our beloved pets were given a first-class burial. Each was carefully wrapped and placed in its own grave, with a marker for its name.

One summer, while we were at Jurata, my father, who often traveled to Vienna, brought back an adorable long-haired basset; we named her Mausi. She became my special friend and took to sleeping in bed with me. This was forbidden, so she would hide under the bed until the lights were out and then jump up and slip in next to me under the covers.

It happened that Mausi had an unplanned pregnancy and gave birth to a litter of mongrels. The puppies were taken away, and while Mausi was still recovering from delivering her large litter, my father took her into the cold waters of the Baltic. The next day she became very sick. My mother learned that there was a good veterinarian at the port of Puck, about twenty kilometers away. As I was too young to travel alone, she took the train with me to see the veterinarian. Mausi had pulmonary congestion, and a battle began to save her life. Every day, I carried the dying dog in a little basket and rode the train to Puck. My mother, who always had nannies and governesses at her disposal, was nevertheless a very devoted parent. She knew how important Mausi was to me, and she went with me every day. It was a tedious journey, for the train stopped at every little station.

At each visit, the veterinarian gave Mausi another shot, but he didn't hold out much hope for her survival. I fed her by hand, forcing her to drink a little bit and making her swallow her pills. Little by little, in spite of pessimistic predictions, Mausi recovered. When my father came home from Warsaw and learned how I had cared for Mausi all those weeks, he simply said, "I am pleased with you." Those were words I didn't hear very often, and I cherished them, as I did the picture of my beloved little dog when, later, cataclysmic events would separate us forever.

Chapter 8

Lessons Out of School

L IKE MOST PARENTS, OUR father saw his children as an extension of himself, and he had grand ambitions for us. We were to receive the best education and training that money could buy, in order to prepare us, both scholastically and socially, to do honor to our family's position in the business and social world. Thus, we were not sent to public school but were provided with private tutors who were devoted entirely to our education. The immediate families, on both sides, were strongly critical of this decision, but our father was determined that we avoid the dubious contacts that were sure to be present in the public schools. It was also his unshakeable conviction that private tutoring would lead to our being superior candidates for advanced studies. This not only proved to be ill-founded, but it also resulted in our being isolated from and ignorant of the real world.

We did, however, have considerable contact with the children of the farm workers, which, if our father had thought about it, were far more dubious contacts than any we were likely to meet in the finer public schools. But perhaps our father discounted them, thinking our social positions were so different that they couldn't have any influence on us.

The boys often accompanied us on hunting excursions. They were hired to find and gather the birds or game that had been killed or wounded. This could be a difficult and sometimes treacherous task, for the reed-filled ponds were hard to penetrate. We used small boats, but often the only practical means was just to wade into the ponds, fighting one's way through the reeds. The boys would do this completely nude. There was always the danger of getting stuck in one of the deep holes that were invisible from the surface, and this could be fatal, even for a good swimmer. The boys, however, were amazingly skilled and never suffered a serious mishap.

We were also dependent upon them when we were hunting in the vast fields and meadows and dense, wild forests. Their agility and initiative became indispensable. The modest amounts of money we paid them for their services seemed to play a minor role in our relationship. It wasn't what appeared to motivate them. Some of them became passionately interested in hunting, even though they played an auxiliary role. This common interest, along with our youth, contributed greatly to establishing a bond between the boys and us. Nevertheless, there remained a barrier that we couldn't cross, for we were at the extreme opposites of the social scale.

We generally talked only about our hunting experiences. Sometimes, though, the conversations were able to lightly stray to other kinds of experiences. It was on one such occasion that I got a vague idea of how babies were made. There is no doubt that these boys, who often slept in the same room with their parents, had a much clearer idea about human reproduction than I did. I had been shielded from any access to information about sex; this was a taboo subject. Our coachman admitted to me one day that my mother had forbidden him to speak to André and me of anything to do with the breeding of horses—a busy enterprise that went on right under our noses at Garbow. We were living so close to animals, and yet with the exception of the dogs, whose unrestrained sex lives couldn't be kept hidden, I had heard and seen nothing to do with the act of reproduction.. Occasionally, after mating, the dogs were not able to separate, and the gardener would throw a bucket of water on them, but somehow, I wasn't able to transpose this uncivilized demonstration of sexual behavior to anything that might be going on in the bedrooms of the refined people in the world I inhabited.

The consequence of my mother's prudishness was that I was entirely ignorant of the anatomy of the female body and how babies actually came about. Her intransigent attitude had its roots in the Polish education system, where the Catholic Church played a primary role. Sexual contact was a sin that one was supposed to confess to the parish priest—probably one of the more difficult sins to confess.

At a time when innumerable women died or were made sterile from maladroit attempts at abortion, performed by inexperienced midwives in lamentably unhygienic conditions, the church helped to at least prevent some women from suffering that calamity by prohibiting sexual relations before marriage. Few people were aware of or had any means to limit pregnancies.

Death in childbirth struck all the social classes with little distinction. Women were tragically vulnerable to dying during pregnancy or childbirth. Use of forceps and caesarean deliveries were unknown. If the fetus couldn't be expelled naturally, both the mother and infant would die. Several Polish queens died in such circumstances. A sad episode, told and retold through several centuries, was of a beloved young queen who was known for her kindness and generosity. As time came for her to deliver her baby, a crowd gathered outside the royal chateau at Krakow and waited for the appearance of a flag that would announce the birth. The waiting was prolonged, and disturbing news began to circulate. Finally, a flag was raised to the top of the chateau, and the crowd uttered a collective gasp of fright and despair. The flag contained not the royal emblem but a skull and crossbones. The queen and her baby had succumbed.

At Stara Wies, the chateau that belonged to my mother's family, a marble statue of the Virgin Saint can be found, along with a moving inscription—a message from Count Krasinski, then the owner of Stara Wies, whose wife died in childbirth at eighteen years of age. The inscription reads: "Our happiness ended this August 25, 1880 ..." and implores the Virgin Saint to unite them again in death.

In the grand salon of the Polish embassy in Washington DC, a beautiful tableau by the famous Polish painter Styka shows King Zygmunt (also spelled as "Sigismont") holding the hand of his suffering wife. The young queen—who was born a Radziwill—died an agonizing death in childbirth.

Much closer to home is my childhood memory of the death of a young woman who worked for our family. When time came for her to give birth, it became apparent that the fetus she was carrying was too large for a normal delivery. The manipulations by the inadequately prepared specialists were to no avail. Her terrifying suffering lasted for two days and ended in death for her and the baby.

Chapter 9

Some Close Calls and a Cure

L OOKING BACK AT MY early years, I consider myself fortunate to have survived. Life and death, at that time, often depended on nothing but luck and the natural defenses of the organism. No amount of wealth could protect one from all the perils of life. In addition, children—boys, in particular—cannot be entirely guarded from foolish and dangerous behavior.

When I was around nine years old, I was quite excited to receive a toy revolver that seemed impressively real. When I pulled the trigger, there was a big bang followed by a flash of light and the odor of gun powder—an actual explosion from little cartridges that contained powder but no bullets. There were succeeding explosions, as each of six cartridges advanced in the magazine.

Not being content to just shoot and make noise to scare the young people in the vicinity, I wanted also to analyze the mechanics and functioning of the revolver. One day, believing that the magazine was empty of cartridges, I attempted to look closely at the action of the magazine by placing one eye just above the opening of the barrel. Unfortunately, one cartridge remained in the gun. I received the charge directly into my eye. Panic ensued. I was seated on the ground, stunned and surrounded by smoke, unable to see clearly. My mother held me and implored frantically, "Get the doctor! Quickly! He could lose an eye!"

There was no car available, and help had to be sought by horseback. Interminable hours of waiting passed before the doctor arrived, in the course of which I was both scolded and consoled. When the doctor finally arrived, he examined my eye through a large glass and concluded that although many particles of powder were encrusted on my cornea, it was best to leave things to nature—that the foreign bodies would be dissolved or rejected without surgical intervention. I was lucky. A less skilled doctor could have caused lasting damage by poking about in my eye. I recovered fully, but the process took a long time.

Among other dramas and tragedies that played out in our young lives, I particularly remember that of a boy who became an expert at throwing marbles in the air and catching them in his mouth. Naturally, the time finally arrived when a marble descended into his throat and became lodged there. The Heimlich method was unknown at that time, and attempts to pry the marble out only pushed it farther down. In a few seconds, the boy lost consciousness, and in several minutes his heart ceased to beat.

Every year we learned of drownings, and once there was even a hanging. A local boy had heard that hanging offers some strange sensations, and he wanted to find out for himself. However, the experiment wasn't interrupted in time, and he didn't live to report on the experience.

It also was not uncommon at that time to lose a child to one of many illnesses that doctors were helpless to treat. My grandmother Gerlicz had nine children, of which three died young. This percentage of around 30 percent was common and could even reach 50 percent among the poor.

One time when I was very sick, my mother had my crib placed beside her bed so that she could watch over me all night. Over the years, I suffered from a number of serious infections that persisted for weeks, sometimes with kidney complications and often with a persistent fever of unknown origin, although fate protected me from any incurable illness.

We had close relatives, however, who were less fortunate. Of the many epidemics, against which there was no remedy, the worst was tuberculosis. My cousin Stanislas Szuman, who was a little older than I, was stricken with this terrible disease. During one vacation season, when he could not leave his room, André and I secretly visited him and sat on his bed, in order to amuse him. He died several months later. All the conditions were present to infect us, but we remained untouched. Later, his younger brother, Josef, died at nine years of age, after suffering a high fever. His agony lasted for days, but the cause was unknown; quite possibly, it was meningitis.

Our parents seemed particularly worried by the thought of tuberculosis. The sole remedy was believed to be the breathing of pure mountain air. André was more delicate than I, and my parents had the disturbing habit of reminding me that André's birth, eleven months after mine, meant that I had gotten the larger share of all that was good, leaving him with the crumbs. The only bit of reality in their concern over André's health was that, unlike me, he suffered often from bronchitis.

I, however, had to suffer from my parents' expectation that André and I should do all the same things at the same time. Therefore, when our parents decided to send André to a mountain resort in the winter months for a "cure," I was dispatched along with him to Rabka, a resort and tuberculosis sanatorium in the Carpates Mountains. We were sent off with our usual impressive entourage: a cook, a maid, and a governess. Unhappily, our parents didn't accompany us.

When we arrived, we saw sick people lying about on terraces, covered in warm furs. We were horrified at the thought of spending our time among these weak and ailing adults. It was not the kind of company two energetic young boys wanted to keep. Fortunately, our parents, as usual, had spared no expense. They had rented a separate villa for us. Thus, we were able to distance ourselves from this depressing spectacle,

Each day, I spent several hours lying on our private terrace, keeping André company, until overcome with boredom, I would wander off to find something to do. My only distraction was a goldfish I had brought with me. I fed it regularly and changed its water. I was sure it knew me and welcomed me when it saw me approaching. Perhaps in my desperation to find something to do, I overfed it. One day, I noticed my little companion wasn't its usual self. I watched helplessly as it gradually expired and floated, lifeless, to the top of the aquarium. I was almost in mourning afterwards.

Gradually, I found some other distractions at Rabka. One, in particular, had a dramatic result. A budding interest in things mechanical and electrical led me to try some experiments with a lamp that had been placed in my room. I removed the light bulb and put a pair of scissors in its place. An enormous spark followed, that melted the blades of the scissors. Then, all was dark—not only in our villa but in the whole vicinity, including the neighboring sanatorium. Finally, after a bit of panic, light was restored. I never admitted responsibility for the incident. Blame was put on the failure to protect for short circuits. Little did I suspect that this first experience with electricity pointed toward a future career.

While at Rabka I discovered another interest that would last a lifetime—I developed a passion for drawing plans. I would draw, in great detail, the objects around me: the furniture, a bedroom, and then a whole house. I dreamed of being a designer of houses and gardens— even entire towns. Two or three years later, I drew a plan of our entire estate, Przybyslawice. Although not of professional quality, it was a design of huge dimensions. When my father saw it, he was impressed. It seemed that, for the first time, he began to take me seriously, as a separate individual with interests and abilities he hadn't recognized or appreciated.

Chapter 10

Hunting and Horses

FROM THE WINDOWS AT Przybyslawice, we had a sweeping view of a broad expanse of reed-covered ponds. Those ponds became our first hunting grounds. By the time André and I were ten years old, we each had guns, but they were small-caliber rifles that could shoot only a short distance. Our main targets were birds, mostly sparrows. We had only middling results, so we didn't leave many dead bodies behind. However, I did have one early success that sticks in my mind. On the branch of a large chestnut tree was perched a beautiful pigeon that had a lovely cooing sound. With my little rifle, I aimed carefully at the pigeon and pulled the trigger. I saw a tuft of feathers burst from its breast, while the pigeon, fluttering crazily, tore away from the branch and disappeared. André, who was beside me, said, "Maybe you wounded it."

"No," I responded with a bit of bravado, "it's probably already dead." Several moments later, a gardener brought me the lifeless pigeon. It had died in flight and fallen to the ground like a stone. The cook promised to make a dish of pigeon for dinner.

When I was older, I would not have wanted to kill that beautiful bird, but at age ten years, I had but one objective—to be a successful hunter. Some of our killing could be justified, because edible game might end up in the kitchen, but less easy to justify was the killing of rare, beautiful specimens just for trophies. The truth is, most hunting was simply for killing, but it was so much our way of life that it took time for my questioning to rise to the surface; I knew nothing else. The entry hall of our home was filled with hunting trophies: antlers of elk, stags, and roe deer; a skin of a bear that my father had killed; birds of prey, including immense eagles and rare specimens of herons; and other aquatic and land birds. I was even responsible for some of these trophies. There was a taxidermist in Lublin that made a fortune, thanks to us. I recognize, today, the mindlessness of this passion for killing, but for quite a while, I was an eager participant.

One particular episode of wanton killing stands out in my mind—and it was all to impress a woman. I wasn't very old, perhaps in my early teens. My parents had invited a friend to visit for several weeks. Our visitor, a Madame Higersberger, was very beautiful. She was either widowed or divorced, and seemed quite elegant and sophisticated, particularly in the way she wore a touch of rouge near the base of her ears. To my disappointment, she ignored me totally. I wanted desperately to get her attention. Then, I had an inspiration. I had noticed that on a tree that neighbored our property, there was a colony of crows. At that time of year, the young were leaving their nests and getting ready to fly away. In order to find them, it would be necessary to get up very early in the morning. At the first light of day, accompanied by a boy named Stasick, who was my age, I went to the tree. There, I began to shoot, creating an uninterrupted cannonade. The crows fell like apples from the tree. I was forced to stop when the two barrels of my shotgun became burning hot. It was carnage. Stasick and I wrapped the dead and dying crows in a cloth brought for the purpose. We deposited the heavy load on the lawn that faced a window, behind which slept the lady I wished to impress. We assembled the cadavers into the shape of an immense heart. This task done, we waited to see the result. After a long wait, the fascinating lady opened her window. Instead of the admiration I expected, I saw terror and disgust on her face. It appeared that I had not made the impression I had hoped for. My parents were not favorably impressed either, and I was reprimanded for my ill-advised attempt to get the attention of their guest.

When I was fourteen years old, Zygmunt and Stefanie came to visit us carrying a mysterious valise. It contained two hunting rifles imported from England—one for André and one for me. This was a present fit for royalty. In truth, we didn't need guns of such quality. Now, we were armed to create a slaughter. Unfortunately, that is what we did. Thanks to my gun, I had some spectacular successes with hunting.

Often, Stefanie was the "queen of the hunt," a title given to the person who killed the most game. She took part in a number of hunting parties organized by the great estates of Poland. Those held at Garbow were known for good organization and the abundance of game. Stefanie was particularly proud of one very special hunting trophy—an extremely rare white heron with green feet. One day she was hunting ducks on a large pond in a very wild area when the heron rose in flight from the reeds. It flew behind her as she was seated in a small boat. It seemed an impossible position but making a desperate effort, she aimed behind her back at the heron. She killed the bird, but she fell with her shotgun into the pond. She managed to retrieve the bird and get to shore with her prize. Although I later had serious misgivings about this love for hunting, I never lost my deep affection for our courageous and adventurous aunt.

A year after we received our new rifles, Stefanie felt that André and I were sufficiently mature and good enough hunters to participate in a hunting party that she had organized at Garbow. For boys of fourteen and fifteen years of age, it was a great privilege to be included. We were to hunt pheasant, partridges, hares, and other animals. Beats were organized in which dozens of village inhabitants, overseen by gamekeepers, would rouse the game by noisily thrashing through their habitat. My performance was lamentable. I had difficulty estimating the difference between the actual position of the bird and the place where I must aim. Stefanie, who observed my difficulties, came to my rescue. She stood not far from me and shot almost simultaneously with me, pretending that I had been the one to succeed in hitting the target. Happily, André saved the family's honor—the results of that day made his talent evident.

Unlike me, André became a serious and sophisticated hunter. He had a formidable helper who often accompanied him—a colossal European owl called a Grand Duc (or *chatillon*). This rare owl is seldom encountered today. It was notorious for raiding and destroying other birds' nests and stealing their eggs. André used the Grand Duc as a lure to attract other birds of prey, such as sparrow hawks and eagles. He would tether the owl to a T-shaped structure, and then he would hide in a specially built blind, which had an opening for his rifle barrel. On seeing the owl, even from far away, birds would swoop in above it, and André would shoot them before they could attack.

The Grand Duc lived in a huge cage—large enough for a man—that had been especially built for it. André was a daily visitor to his owl, taking it raw meat and live mice that he raised just for that purpose. He succeeded in taming the owl sufficiently so that he could enter the cage without fear and take the bird out on hunting parties. I never dared to touch the Grand Duc—his powerful claws could easily have crushed a boy's arm. Furthermore, hunting with the owl didn't interest me very much, for I didn't have the patience to wait for hours in a blind. André, like Stefanie, had a natural affinity for hunting and outdoor adventure.

Hunting was never a way of life for me. From an early age, I began filling my school notebooks with numbers and averages and correlations between the number of cartridges fired and the particular species killed. This work interested me more than the hunt itself. A teacher worthy of his or her calling would have noticed this interest and advised my parents to focus my studies in that direction. Unfortunately, this was only one example of our tutors many shortcomings which would later come to light.

Some of the first stirrings of my eventual distaste for hunting may have started with a critical article that appeared in the press. My father was a very expert hunter. He possessed a veritable arsenal of shotguns of different calibers for different uses, which were on display in a large cabinet. As his business pursuits took more and more of his time, he participated only in exceptional hunts devoted to large game. By the beginning of the twentieth century, bears were becoming rare in Poland, but there was still a colony in the eastern Carpates Mountains on the border of Romania. So my father went there to hunt bear. He spent several cold nights in a blind, hung above ground in a tree, with the dead body of a cow below him to serve as bait. He eventually got his bear—the skin was his most prized trophy. At this time, there were no protected species in Poland. Ignorant hunters, like us, were able to contribute to the decline of wild animals, almost to the point of extinction. I remember the exact words I read in the press: *znow padiniedzwiedz* ("Again, a bear has fallen").

Another experience profoundly affected my feelings about killing animals. It was on a hunting party organized for André and me by one of our father's friends, a Mr. Wyganowski, a landholder and industrialist who was on several boards of directors with our father. It was only some years later that I learned the probable reason for his generosity. He was notorious for his prodigious sexual appetite, which he freely indulged with his servants, as well as women of his own social standing. After his marriage, he had to become more discreet. He made frequent trips to Warsaw under the pretext of attending board meetings. When his wife tried to reach him by telephone, my father's secretary would say that he was attending an important meeting. In return for this favor, Mr. Wyganowski supported my father in business meetings. It was probably in the same spirit that he organized the hunt. He even accompanied us personally. We drove to the hunt in his carriage, with a servant preceding us, carrying a bucket of candies. When the children of a village appeared, our host held the bucket and threw candies to them. This grandiose performance did not impress me favorably. Indeed, I found such an insensitive display of largesse toward those he presumed to be his inferiors quite embarrassing.

Later, Mr. Wyganowski's questionable character came under serious scrutiny when he somehow persuaded my father to buy a very expensive mare from his son. The horse was given to me as a present and quickly succeeded in almost killing me. When I mounted the horse for the first time, I rode around in front of the house, first trotting, and then galloping. My mother was on the steps, watching me. Suddenly, the horse jumped high into the air, while executing a powerful kick. I instantly found myself airborne. I was thrown so high and so hard that I spun in a circle, turned upside down, and plunged head-first toward the gravel-covered path. I can still recall that plunge and seeing the ground approaching. Curiously, the impact produced no pain. After that, there is only a dim memory of my mother's rushing toward me and bending close, her face contorted in fear. And then, nothing. I woke up, stretched out on a couch, surrounded by my parents and several servants. A car had been sent for a doctor. I rose up and tried to move, but I couldn't walk straight. When the doctor finally arrived, he was able to do little but confirm the obvious—I had suffered a concussion. At that time, scanners didn't exist, so we didn't know if anything had happened to my brain. Soon, I was able to walk normally again, but for quite a while I felt nauseated and dizzy at the slightest jolt. Little by little, over a period of months, I recovered. An inquiry was made concerning the horse, and it was discovered that it was subject to unpredictable attacks of madness, during which blood ran from its nostrils. Mr. Wyganowski must have known of its dangerous behavior.

While the experience with the horse was yet ahead of me, my hunting experience on Mr. Wyganowski's estate was also fraught with drama. During the hunt, someone pointed out a roe deer with spectacular antlers. Although it was quite a distance away, I aimed carefully and fired. The animal instantly collapsed. With two rural guards at my side, who were responsible for policing the forest, I approached the deer. It suddenly rose up and bounded toward me, uttering terrifying screams. One of the guards had the presence of mind to grab at the deer's antlers as it was charging, and he succeeded in holding it while the other guard fired at point-blank range, killing the deer instantly. This scene left a strong impression on me—not because of the danger of being injured by the charging deer but because when I'd found myself in such close proximity to this beautiful animal, I fully realized, for the first time, what suffering I caused. Until then, I had not given much thought to the physical pain the hunter was inflicting upon his fellow creatures. I had mainly hunted birds and small game, such as rabbits. They die almost in silence, allowing the hunter to ignore the suffering he causes. I was to have no regrets when I could no longer hunt. Today, when I see men carrying guns to go hunting, it stirs uncomfortable feelings in me.

Although my experience with the deer was something of an epiphany, my hunting days did not come to an end. It is hard to imagine what my family's reaction would have been if I had suddenly renounced that lifestyle. Instead, I spent more and more of my time riding horses, while André devoted himself to hunting. With our coachman as a frequent companion, I would go for long rides in the forests. Sometimes, we would take off the horses' saddles and let them roam free for a while. This didn't always work out well, for they became a little wild and could be difficult to retrieve. My favorite of our horses was Kitka, an intelligent mare that was obstinate on occasion. Because she was a purebred Anglo-Arabian, my uncle Zygmunt wanted to breed her. That created a problem for me, for when Kitka had a foal, she didn't want to leave the stable. When finally she was persuaded to leave, she would try to head back home at every turn in the road. It was a struggle to keep her going the way I wanted to go. Another more serious problem was that she was afraid of motor vehicles. Indeed, they were still so rare in those days that many accidents occurred when frightened horses bolted at the passage of a car. But Kitka learned a little trick. When an automobile appeared on the horizon, she would turn herself so the car would pass behind her. At first I was surprised and frightened. Then I learned to let her handle the situation. This exemplified something often said—that a rider didn't even need to think— that the horse would do that for him. Indeed, horses were such an integral part of Polish culture that it was said that riders, much like the American cowboy, could live on their horses, eating and even sleeping in the saddle.

Chapter 11

Hunters and the Hunted

I T WAS IN THE mid-1930s when our family made two memorable
trips to the wild forests and marshes of eastern Poland. The trips
were partly for hunting and partly for sightseeing. The first trip
was to the immense forests of Bialowieza in northeastern Poland. These
forests had once covered much of Europe. They were left in a virgin
state for centuries and were still remarkably untouched. The absence of
people allowed a rich variety of rare animal and bird species to prosper.
Certain species of birds lived there that had become extinct elsewhere.
Bears had been there from the beginning of time. Huge black oxen
survived in Bialowieza for years after they became extinct in Europe.
(The last of their number disappeared in the seventeenth century.)

The Russians had controlled Bialowieza during the time of the
czars. After the cataclysmic events of the First World War and the
Russian Revolution, Poland regained control of its forests. But in what
state? Pristine areas had been marked by the ravages of war, and the
huge bison that had lived there—cousins of the buffalo that once
roamed the American plains—had almost all been wiped out. They
had been killed by the deserters from the two armies that clashed
there: the Russians and the Germans. Luckily, after the war, the Polish
authorities were able to gather bison in various European zoos and in a
few decades, a colony of well-protected bison developed.

We explored the forests by car and on foot, and the spectacle was unforgettable. This natural setting had been largely untouched since the glacier age. Some trees had attained colossal dimensions, and those that had been vanquished by age spread across wide swaths of ground, covering and being covered by dense undergrowth. The bison were now in a well-guarded preserve where access was forbidden. The guards must have taken us as important dignitaries because of our impressive car and the way our chauffeur, Budrys, who was very dignified, waved his hand in a gesture that indicated they should let us pass. Thus, we were able to approach close to the herd of bison and to admire those living vestiges of prehistoric times.

While at Bialowieza, we stayed in the hunting lodge of the last czar. It was actually a huge palace, surrounded by a large park, which had been able to comfortably accommodate the czar and his entourage. The notorious Marshall Goering, Hitler's closest henchman, often hunted there and stayed in the same lodge. In fact, in 1933, Goering became Master of the German Hunt and of the German Forests. As a result, Bialowieza was not decimated during World War II because Goering had given orders to spare the region.

While walking near the lodge, I noticed a dog of impressive size. The workers told us, "That's Goering's dog. He left it in our care." I approached the dog to pet him, but he showed me some very impressive teeth. My reaction was, "Here is a mean dog that belongs to a *boche* (a pejorative term for Germans), so they can both die." I didn't really wish the dog ill, nor could I have actually anticipated the events that would come to pass.

Goering, the great hunter and Nazi war criminal (as well as pillager of art, not only in Poland but in France), was condemned to die at the Nuremburg trials after World War II ended. However, he succeeded in poisoning himself the night before his scheduled execution. If his dog still lived, perhaps he found a kinder owner.

After seeing the forests of Bialowieza, our second trip, the following year, was to the marshes of Prypec. These were the most important marshes in Europe and covered hundreds of square miles. They were situated in eastern Poland on either side of the Prypec River. This river was fed by numerous tributaries and meandered slowly in many loops before it finally entered the Dniepr in Russian territory. The marshes were also home to rare species not found anywhere else in Europe.

It was on that trip that we witnessed a sad little drama. We took the route that connected Warsaw to Pinsk, the main town in that area. This was a strategic route, which was supposed to be able to assure the passage of armies. It was kept in as good condition as was possible at that period of time. However, there were still few cars in Poland, and we found it totally empty. For dozens of miles, we encountered nothing more than a peasant cart. In this marsh region, cultivated ground was rare, so there were few inhabitants. As we passed by one meadow, a strange spectacle drew our attention. A young girl, who had been tending to a flock of sheep, was being attacked by a goat. This furious animal was butting her with his head as he chased her about the meadow. We stopped the car, and everything happened very quickly. My father, accompanied by Budrys, who was armed with a cane that he always had in the trunk, "just in case," rushed to defend the young shepherdess. Budrys struck the goat on the head with a mighty whack, and the bad-tempered animal ran off. This done, our attention turned to the girl. She couldn't have been more than twelve years of age at the most. She was quite tiny and pale and was crying softly. She didn't appear to be wounded, but certainly she had to be bruised by the many blows from the goat. She told us that this was not the first time the goat had attacked her. What could we do in this circumstance? My mother tried to calm and console the child, while my father did the only thing he could think of—he took out some bills and put them in the girl's apron pocket. It was not a large sum for us, but in that region of great poverty, it would have been a significant windfall. That done, we continued on our trip. I tried to imagine the astonishment of the girl's family when she told them of her experience and showed them her little fortune.

As we continued our journey, the region became more and more wild. We spent the night in the largest of several modest thatch cottages. In the *izba*, or main room, of this peasant house, we were surprised to see clippings of American newspapers nailed to the walls. Later, we learned that the United States ambassador had stayed there in the same cottage, when he was on a hunting trip.

For the villagers, the newspaper clippings were something to treasure and display. For us, it showed their poverty and isolation. It seemed to disturb my father. I remember his commenting that we had "too much poverty in our country" and that "it should be remedied."

He said he hoped the ambassador had fully compensated the peasant for his hospitality.

When we left this poor and humble hotel, we traveled using a horse-drawn cart; in those places that were less accessible, we went by foot. Only the most insensitive visitor could have failed to admire the wild beauty of this region.[11] It was an unforgettable countryside, with immense, almost impenetrable marshes, surrounded by woods, and filled with the slowly winding tributaries of the Prypec River. Some of the marshes were covered with great, tall reeds, while others couldn't be easily distinguished from the undergrowth. The often-dense vegetation was reflected in the waters of the many tributaries. The entire region, much of it inaccessible to humans, constituted a natural reserve for innumerable species of aquatic birds, such as rare geese and herons, and the *slomki,* a bird glorified by the poet Mickiewicz.

It pains me now to write that we were there to kill some of those birds. I was placed at the edge of a stretch of water that was partly covered by reeds, where there were a number of ducks. I had a whistle in my pocket that could almost exactly replicate the call of a female duck. The males were easily attracted. All I had to do was shoot them, but I was not very successful. I was better at imitating the ducks' call than killing them. During our stay there, André killed a rare goose and, sadly, I killed a beautiful *slomki.* These were added to our collection and regarded as some of our most interesting trophies.

During the Second World War, the Prypec Marshes became a perfect refuge for the Soviet partisans. They were able to hide there with impunity and emerge to launch attacks against their enemies. It was treacherous to try to follow them back into the marshes, for the uninitiated would risk drowning. The water was deep and covered with aquatic plants. With one false step, one could be swallowed up and be unable to fight one's way back to the surface.

---

11   None of this region is in Poland today. The Soviet Union annexed it in 1945, at the end of World War II. After the breakup of the Soviet Union, the Prypec Marshes became part of Belorussia in the north and the Ukraine in the south.

Chapter 12
Warsaw—No. 25 Mokotowska

FROM THE TIME I was about five years old, my mother and brother and I spent part of each winter in Warsaw at No. 25 Mokotowska, where my grandfather Bohdan Broniewski had his residence and the administrative offices for all the businesses he directed, including the varied enterprises at Garbow. Upon Bohdan's death, my father took over. He used the second floor for business offices, and we lived on the first floor during our winters there. It was a beautiful residence—actually, a little palace. It consisted of a main building and two annexes—one annex housed the chauffeur and garage, the other housed the gardener. The three buildings surrounded a beautifully landscaped courtyard of lush vegetation, flower beds, and many trees.

Around 1928, when I was six years old, my father moved the business offices to a separate location and hired a renowned architect, Antoni Jawornicki, to transform No. 25 Mokotowska into a suitably grand family residence. While the renovation was going on, if we weren't at Garbow, we stayed at the Bristol Hotel. It was considered the finest hotel in Warsaw and, not surprisingly, my father was on its board of directors. A photo exists of him and Mr. Jawornicki seated together during a gala dinner at the Bristol.

Hotel life for young boys who were used to having acres of ground available for play and exploration was miserable. I sneaked a small dog into our rooms and kept it hidden, but it announced its presence by leaving several messes. The dog was banished back to Garbow.

One evening, while the residence was still under construction, we visited the site with our mother. We went upstairs via a stairway from the servants' quarters. We didn't see the large hole, where a serpentine stairway to the second floor was still to be built. It was covered with paper and not visible. I fell through the hole but saved myself from crashing to the ground floor by reaching out and grabbing at a cement slab that was between the two floors. I hung there precariously, while my frantic mother quickly rounded up rescuers to get me back to earth.

When the reconstruction was finally finished, we were able to escape our hotel prison and move into No. 25 Mokotowska. No expense had been spared. The entire interior was done in art deco style, which was quite in vogue at that time in western Europe, particularly in France. Most of the furniture and rugs had been imported, and of the twenty or more paintings, a number were by famous artists and of museum quality.[12] The total effect was spectacular.

A modest-sized entryway was all in marble: white marble for the floors, and black marble with veins of white for the walls. From the entryway one stepped through a grand portal that opened to reveal the elegant, serpentine stairway to the second floor.

Two dining rooms were on the second floor: an intimate one with a marble fireplace for small gatherings and family dining, and a much larger one with three chandeliers that hung over a table large enough to comfortably seat thirty people. There was a small salon for small gatherings and a larger salon for receptions. There was also a study, which was reserved mainly for men, and next to that was the largest

---

12   There were paintings by two Polish artists of international reputation: *Anthony and Cleopatra* and *Sprzedaz Amuletow* (The Selling of Amulets) by Henryk Siemiracki (1843–1902), and two works by Jan Styka (1858–1925): *Neron,* and *Eunice with Petronius.* It was this latter painting that impressed me enormously. It was taken from a scene in *Quo Vadis,* the work of the great Polish novelist Sienkiewicz, who received a Nobel Prize in 1905. The painting represents an elegant setting in a Roman palace during the persecution of the first Christians by the emperor Nero. The figures of Petronius and Eunice are nude and almost life-sized. They have cut their veins to commit suicide and are lying side by side in an embrace, as their blood blends together. The painting was hung in a special alcove in the entry and was lighted in a fashion that accentuated the luminous quality and striking contrast of their skin coloring. These paintings, along with all the others, were the victims of pillaging during and after World War II. Many were stolen and carried away by the Nazi occupants. Over the course of the years, certain paintings reappeared in auctions and museums.

room of all, with enough space for people to dance. I remember several elegant receptions that were attended by important people from the worlds of finance, industry, and politics.

A wrinkled and torn photo of those halcyon days survives that shows my parents in evening clothes, seated in a salon. My father discovered it when he returned to Warsaw after the war and found his once-beautiful mansion in deplorable condition. On the photo, he wrote a dedication to my mother: "Found in the basement among the debris, I send you, dear Zophia, this photo, which will bring back to you memories of the splendid times of our life: Warsaw, December 15, 1947."

The third floor of the mansion contained a library and our parents' bedrooms. My mother and father each had an apartment that included a wardrobe and a bathroom, as well as a dressing room for my mother and exercise room for my father. The fourth floor had servants' rooms and utility rooms and a large bedroom and two bathrooms for André and me.

In 1929, when I was seven and one-half years old, our sister, Marysia, was added to the family. A huge room, much larger than André's and mine, was next to our mother's room, and it was given to Marysia. This was just one sign of what our sister herself would later admit—that she was quite spoiled. From the beginning, when she was just in her cradle, she occupied a very large space in our family, both literally and figuratively. This, no doubt, was because our parents felt blessed to have a little girl, and also because that little girl had a very strong personality, which was evident before she could even talk. Our father, who was so strict with his sons, was very indulgent toward his daughter and lavished presents upon her. Her wardrobe was filled with expensive clothes from the best shops in Warsaw, London, Paris, and Vienna. Her room held hundreds of dolls and several dollhouses. It was furnished in French provincial, and the walls were hung with exquisite English aquarelles that illustrated Victorian fairy tales. Many were genuine works of art. Somehow, she survived this overindulgence and grew up to be a successful author.

One might wonder why Marysia had such a large and elegant room, while André and I had to share a room. A sudden burst of frugality did not overtake our father once construction reached the fourth floor. Rather, it was his conviction that André and I should be treated much like twins, and it never occurred to him that we might want separate rooms. However, we were hardly confined to a cramped garret on the fourth floor while Marysia lived in splendor below. Our room was quite large, and when I experienced the budding of what would become a lifetime interest in woodworking, our parents had a room next to our bedroom especially equipped for this hobby.

The first floor of the mansion included the kitchen and various servants' rooms, as well as a fully equipped classroom with a large blackboard for André and me. Later, a second classroom was added for Marysia—her schooling consisted of classes held with a specially selected group of girls. She remembered her teachers as being a respectable covey of well-intentioned but uninspiring old ladies.

For all the splendor of our life in Warsaw, it was very confining compared to life at Garbow. When we were little, we couldn't venture beyond our own premises without a nanny. As we grew older, we still didn't have the same freedom or options to go far afield in Warsaw as we did in Garbow. Fortunately, Warsaw had some magnificent parks, some that were quite close to where we lived. One, the immense Lazienki Park, had been the royal residence in the eighteenth century for the last Polish king, Stanislaw Poniatowski. The Renaissance Italian-style palace was surrounded with ponds and fountains and sculptures set among lush verdure. Somewhere in that beautiful park, however, was a cold and gloomy path. The first time we went to Lazienki Park, I suddenly needed to go to the bathroom. Because I was too shy to tell this to our young nanny, I wet my pants. Naturally, I was scolded. The next time we returned to that path, just like Pavlov's dog, I experienced the same urge. After several incidents, the nanny complained to our mother, "Every time he squeezes my hand, he goes pee pee." My mother, who was far more understanding, didn't scold me. How much happier I would have been, much of the time, if I could have known the tender and kind ministrations of my mother, instead of that of hired help.

Chapter 13

Servants and Friends

THERE CAN BE NO doubt that all the servants and workers at our different dwellings allowed us to enjoy a life of great ease, and wherever we went, a staff accompanied us to allow us to maintain the same lifestyle away from home. It was also true that although we were absolutely dependent upon all the people who served us, they brought with them a broad array of human relations problems. There was no lack of dissension, jealousy, infidelity, intrigue, dishonesty, thefts, and fights, as well as serious illnesses, marriages, births, and deaths. It was impossible for us to be unaware of or uninvolved in all these human dramas.

Overall, owners were able to count on the loyalty and devotion of their servants. One example of this devotion stands out in my memory. A young girl, probably a kitchen helper, returned to the house from the icebox where she had put some perishable food. As she passed by my father, she kissed his hand. He made a slight friendly motion with his head. This spontaneous display of respect and esteem toward the master of the house was very common in the Polish countryside. Poland hadn't known the revolution "a la Francaise," which pitted the people against the privileged classes. In Poland, entire families—often for several generations—were attached to the service of the same estate.

My father gave particular concern to the children of the workers. He introduced an innovation that was probably the first in Poland—a one-month summer camp for the children of all the workers at the establishments he controlled. He personally organized this so that all the children were well fed and spent their time agreeably and healthfully. Years later, our family received emotionally moving and nostalgic letters of appreciation from former workers; and we followed the lives of those who had been closest to us.

Francoise, one of our longest term and most loyal employees and someone to whom we were much attached, stayed in Warsaw during the war to watch over our property. This was a brave but foolhardy decision. She would not survive the war.

Francoise's sister, Sophie, who stayed at Przybyslawice during the war, died of food poisoning. This was the final episode in poor Sophie's life. She had married a young man that we knew well, as he also worked for us. My parents organized their marriage, arranged a place for them to live, and gave them a cow to get their married life off to a good start. Several months later, Sophie's husband contracted diphtheria. Immunizations against that awful disease were not yet available in Poland. Diphtheria expresses itself in a strong inflammation of the pharynx and a swelling of membranes that can suffocate the invalid. A surgical intervention to open the respiratory canal might save the patient, but doctors in Poland were not as advanced as their counterparts in a number of other countries. My parents called in a doctor from Warsaw, but he was able to do nothing for Sophie's husband. I took a forbidden look into the sick room and could see the frightening effect of diphtheria; after that, I didn't want to look again. Sophie's husband soon died of suffocation.

That was not the end of Sophie's troubles. Several years later, she married one of our gardeners. This handsome man was involved with many of the girls who worked for us. Sophie came crying to my mother and, by chance, I was present for the severe reprimand my mother gave to her husband. I am not sure if her remonstrations, citing the suffering he was causing Sophie and exhorting him to uphold his marriage vows, had the desired result, for Sophie became even sadder.

Each evening, Sophie washed my feet while telling me interesting stories. I looked forward immensely to this daily ritual and tried to prolong the pleasure by getting her to tell more stories. But the day came when she no longer had the heart to go on with our little routine, and I, too, was sad, for I missed our intimate time together. Years later,

I heard that her unfaithful husband had drowned in one of the ponds at Garbow.

One of the less sympathetic characters in our domestic dramas was Mademoiselle Anna Malachowska. She was around thirty-five years old, blonde, and quite pretty. Anna's family was originally from eastern Poland—territories that had been occupied by the Bolsheviks during the First World War. Her family was forced to flee their land. They took what was perhaps the last boat leaving Crimea for the free countries. Anna had been warmly recommended to my mother by a family friend. She was hired to serve as a companion for André and me in order to perfect our French, and to be available sometimes to take care of Marysia.

I was ten years old when Anna appeared on the scene. Until that time, I was always accompanied on my horseback riding by our coachman. One day, I was pleased to find that the coachman had been replaced by someone much younger—Mlle Anna Malachowska. I owe a debt to Anna—as well as to my aunt Stefanie—for my becoming a skillful rider. Anna's talent at riding—and perhaps her stunning physique—must have been the inspiration for my father to take up horseback riding. I had never seen him on a horse, so it was quite a surprise when he joined Anna and André and me on our outings. I understand today why my mother didn't appreciate these adventures.

Anna had one ambition—to marry a rich man. An exceptional opportunity presented itself in the person of Tade Karso-Siedlewski, my father's best friend. Tade was around forty years old and very rich. In addition to his personal fortune, he had inherited a well-known beer-making enterprise from an aunt. Tade had a property at Kostancin, a residential quarter near Warsaw that was known for its antiques and treasures. I had the occasion to admire them without understanding their importance.

Tade, who was privileged financially and socially, had a problem attracting women. It was generally agreed that this was because he was rather ugly. He had a face so fat and red that people compared him to a well-nourished young pig. Unfortunately, the body that went with the face did nothing to improve the picture. His difficulties with romance also had another source—his taste in women far exceeded his extremely limited charms. He didn't want a woman of modest accomplishments.

He was searching for a more flamboyant woman—worldly and possibly famous. Our very attractive Anna did not live up to his standards.

Finally, he found what he was looking for—a beautiful and famous actress. He smothered her with presents, and she became his mistress. He followed this success with a proposal of marriage. After much reticence, she accepted. A grand marriage was planned. Before the wedding, Tade went to see my father and said, "You know, there is nothing between my fiancée and me now. This is because she is waiting for us to be married in order to make a difference." My father looked straight into his friend's eyes and said to him, "Tade, I believe that you are crazy." It was years later, when I was old enough to understand, that my father related this story to me.

My parents helped with Tade's wedding, to which all the elite of society were invited. The ceremony went well, but afterwards, at the reception, the bride excused herself for a short time. While the guests were waiting for her, Tade did his best to occupy them. But as the wait became prolonged, he stood looking out the window, saying nothing. Finally, the bride appeared, her dress looking a bit rumpled. The couple left on their honeymoon that same evening. At each new hotel, as they traveled, a basket of flowers awaited the young bride. The honeymoon became an abominable masquerade for Tade. On their return, the marriage was annulled. The actress chose love over money and married a landowner of considerably less fortune.

After this terrible misadventure, Tade visited us more often than he had in the past. He confided to my mother that no woman would ever interest him until the end of his life. Thus, Anna's advances were of no avail. But Anna's reign was coming to an end. As soon as an opportunity presented itself, my mother got rid of her. She was given a generous compensation and a promise to recommend her to some friends. Anna made a last tentative appeal to my father who wisely choose not to contradict his wife's decision. Tade, we later learned with sadness, was killed during the first days of the bombardment of Warsaw in September 1939.

Chapter 14
A New Locale and New Times

FROM AN EARLY AGE, we were made to understand that all cultivated Poles must speak French. It was the "language of the salon." Our lessons for this language of the aristocracy took place under an exquisite arbor, surrounded by lawn and flowerbeds. I grew to hate that arbor, which I forever after associated with the tedium of hours spent learning by heart the rules of French grammar. I memorized them without any comprehension and remained always stubbornly ignorant. However, the comprehension I acquired of the spoken language was to serve me well later.

Our home schooling did have some practical advantages. We were not restrained by fixed hours or schedules, as the teachers came to us. Moreover, our teachers accompanied us on vacations which, at least in our father's mind, were "study vacations." I particularly remember one skiing vacation when we were fairly young. Each day after skiing, we were supposed to attend lessons, but André was so tired that all he could do was cry. Wherever we vacationed, however, whether the mountains or the seaside, our lessons took second place. Most of our tutors did not seem to mind. It was a vacation for them also.

It wasn't until André and I were in our mid-teens that we started attending public school. Until that time, we were free to take long skiing vacations in the winter. When we went on many such vacations at Zakopane, we were accompanied by our ever-faithful Francoise, another maid or two, our indispensable cook, and our tutors.

While everyone enjoyed this little arrangement, we were living an illusion, particularly our father. Even when I was still quite young, I began to suspect that our education was falling short of expectations, particularly in the sciences. Finally, there was a hard awakening for our parents. The law required that once we reached a certain age, we must take an examination. The results were a disaster. Taking into account my father's prominent position, the director of the high school in Warsaw met with him personally to give him the results: we were weak in all subjects, particularly mathematics. Even in French spelling, we were hopeless—and we had French speakers living with us who were responsible for teaching us their language. Our stunned parents asked themselves how this could have happened. Were their sons stupid? They quickly discarded this possibility. The responsibility must fall upon the tutors. Had this occurred deliberately, they wondered, or because of laziness or negligence? In the case of one tutor whose politics made him hostile toward the wealthy class, it well may have been deliberate.

Our parents had no alternative but to enroll us at a high school in Warsaw. The first days were a nightmare. All the students had known each other since they started school. We were strangers with strange ways, never having learned the give-and-take of the social milieu in which we found ourselves. Each high school had a special cap that the students wore to distinguish them from the students at the other schools. It was very important to wear this misshapen cap in a certain fashion, which we learned only after being thoroughly humiliated by wearing it incorrectly. But after a while, the other students began to accept us, and in general, we found our fellow students to be sympathetic and often well-raised, contrary to our father's expectations.

For me, the school experience was rewarding. I was soon able to catch up with others in my class and then found myself progressing rapidly. Mathematics became a passion, and I began to excel. My only competition to that point had been André, who was younger than I and had difficulties with some of his studies. Now, I was faced with boys my age, and I experienced intense competition for the first time. I felt driven to try to be the top in the class. I ended up sharing top honors with another student named Jablonski, but I was better than he in mathematics, a subject highly regarded in Poland. Our school was ranked as one of the best, and the director was the mathematics professor. He was very demanding, and I was extremely happy at the end of the school year when he complimented me, saying, "I didn't expect this to happen." My father was also surprised, not only by my success itself but in how my success compared to André's performance. For the first time, his assumption that André would be his successor in the business world, while I went into agriculture, began to come into question.

Once we entered public school, we lived in Warsaw most of the time. In the early to mid-1930s, a sudden passion for aviation took place in western Europe, particularly in France and Great Britain. Poland followed, in a modest way. Close to Mokotowska Street was a large field that the city of Warsaw decided to turn into an airfield. Always accompanied by a parent or someone from the household staff, André and I would go often to see the aerodrome. With a bit of luck, we would occasionally see a little airplane take off or land—this was very exciting. At home, I cut out model airplanes from paper and hung them from the ceiling of our bedroom.

My father, always interested in the latest form of progress, began to interest himself in this new means of transport. He came close to buying his own airplane from an English company that lured him to England to visit their plant. He returned from this trip very impressed. I can still hear him explaining the testing of the motors to our mother, telling her, "Those motors can never break down."

In order to get us children on his side, the manufacturer proposed to take André and me for a ride in his airplane. This was high adventure for us. Our parents were there to watch us take off. As our little plane taxied across the field and picked up more speed, it began to roll. The faster we went, the worse it got. I could see the ground rising and falling outside the windows as we pitched and tumbled our way down the field. Suddenly, the pilot jerked the plane abruptly to one side to avoid an unexpected obstacle. A long stick, planted in the field, pierced one wing of the plane, and we jolted to a stop. That was the end of our flight. Given the erratic behavior of the plane while still on the ground, it seemed far better to have had an accident there than after takeoff.

This was a viewpoint that resonated with our mother. While our father continued to envision buying an airplane and having our chauffeur, Budrys, fly it (heaven knows what Budrys would have thought of that), our mother intervened forcefully, "In a car, if the motor stops, you can park at the side of the road; in an airplane, it is a catastrophe. And to use an airplane, you have to have places to land. Where are the airfields?" Our father grudgingly agreed, but he didn't give up the idea of flying. He seized every opportunity, limited as they were, to travel by plane—and, if circumstances permitted, to transport his family the same way.

Thus, André and I became air travelers at a very young age. One episode remains vivid in my memory. We were flying from the port of Gdynia, situated at the edge of the Baltic Sea, to Warsaw. My family and some friends, the Regulskis, took our seats in a single-engine plane of German manufacture. The weather was bad and after some delay, the pilot reluctantly took off. While in the air, a storm broke out, and the pilot had to divert from his course. Even when the worst of the storm passed, it continued to rain, and our pilot lost his way. There either were no radio communications at that time or they were of poor quality. When a town came into view, the pilot tried to find out where we were by flying low over the train station. He flew lower and lower, going in circles, trying to read the name of the town that was always on the outside of the station. I am convinced the Regulskis and our family were close to death at that moment. Without the lifting force of air beneath the plane, we could have dropped like a stone. But we survived and arrived in Warsaw hours past schedule.

Another memorable flight occurred when my father sent André and me and a governess, Mlle Gomulinska, on a flight to Poznan. A very strong wind was blowing from west to east, against the flight of our plane. The pilot decided to fly very low, at fifty meters, to avoid the full force of the wind. At that altitude, the plane shook violently, and André and poor Mlle Gomulinska were sick from the beginning to the end of the flight. I took this opportunity to cruelly tease our governess, who was trying to hide her condition. Neither she nor André wanted to get into the plane for the return flight, but I argued with them and eventually won. The return flight was much calmer, as were the stomachs of my fellow passengers.

In the mid 1930s, Poland began to modernize in many areas. Soon after building the airfield, the first golf course was built, just to the east of Warsaw. Naturally, my father decided he had to take up golf. As this was a very snobbish sport, it was necessary to be properly outfitted. The best clubs and an entire wardrobe, including the shoes and the cap, were ordered from London. The result was impressive. My father looked just like an English gentleman. The entire family accompanied him to the golf course for the first golfing experience. Everything was ready for the first stroke—a boy carried the clubs, and the ball was placed on the tee. I don't know if my father had taken golf lessons, but he was unable to hit the ball. Witnessing his difficulties, an employee approached him and said, "Here, let me show you how to do it." He took the club and, swinging mightily, he exhibited both power and style. Unfortunately, he also missed the ball. Instead, he hit the ground with such force that he tore up a large tuft of grass. Rain had fallen recently, so the grass was accompanied by dripping mud. Alas, the mud got all over my father's beautiful new clothes and even splattered onto his face. I was not able to control myself and burst into laughter. My father was furious, and he scolded, "You have no respect for your parents!" I was never invited to watch him play golf again, but I suspect that he abandoned the sport.

Chapter 15

Time Plays Out

IN THE WINTER OF 1939, we had what was to be our last skiing trip.
We went to Zakopane in southeastern Poland, which was situated
in the massive Tatras Mountains, the highest range (over 8,500
feet) in the Carpathian mountain range. The resort was surrounded
with high plateaus, mountain pastures, and hills covered with forests
of pine. It was a very wild area. The mountain people who inhabited
the region were called *gorals*. They lived on the resources of the land
and raised sheep and cows. They also created beautiful handicrafts:
embroidered clothes for men and women, linens, tapestries, and even
some furs. Their wood sculptures were of high artistic value and were
exported all over the world.

We hired a goral for his horses, his sleighs, his warm blankets, and
especially for his knowledge of the mountains. Unfortunately, he and
our cook got into some serious altercations. She was a formidable person
to deal with, both because of her temperament and her size. She was
quite fat and had a mean disposition. The gorals were a proud people
and not of a mind to be pushed around by a fat cook—and a woman
at that. It required all of my mother's skill and patience to keep their
disputes at a low simmer.

Each morning our goral would take four people to the slopes in his
sleigh. Sometimes skiers were pulled by a horse or sleigh. This was called
ski-joring, a very popular sport at that time. André and I would *ski-jor*

behind the sleigh. With nothing to do but hang on, we could admire the views of the sharp, granite summits of the Tatras and the famous high-mountain lake, Morskie Oko ("eye of the sea"), which reflected the vertical walls of the Tatras.

That last year at Zakopane was the most exciting because the first chair lift in Poland had been installed. It was both exciting and dangerous—Zakopane had no slopes for beginners, so everyone had to take the chair lift to the summit and descend on the same slopes—this resulted in many accidents. An acquaintance of my parents had his rib cage pierced by a ski pole.

This new challenge led to my parents hiring a ski instructor, who was responsible for my making great progress. I even tried some ski jumping but was put to shame by the mountain children who, at less than ten years of age, could far outdo my efforts. Our ski instructor, who participated in international championship events, was very good-looking. He boasted that the women of high society, to whom he gave private lessons, needed some "distraction." Apparently, rich and idle women did not disdain a little adventure and were often vulnerable to his charms.

Perhaps this was the case with *Borsuk,* a woman who was staying with her son in a chalet close to ours. *Borsuk,* in Polish, means badger, and as everybody knows, the badger is a cute little animal with long hair that is used for shaving brushes. André, who always knew how to find the most expressive names, called this woman "Borsuk" because of a little too much hair on her face. Other than that, she was not unattractive. Somehow, she managed to impose her presence on my parents, especially my father—she succeeded in drawing him into her skiing trips. My mother did not appreciate this. It wasn't enough that she spent much of her vacation time overseeing a household of children and servants. She also had to break up fights between her cook and the goral and keep a predatory badger away from her husband.

The summer of 1939 was also to be our last time at Jurata, the resort on the Baltic where we had a villa. Jurata was situated on the Hel Peninsula, a thin stretch of land, no more than one kilometer wide, that ran parallel to the shore for almost twenty kilometers. It separated the Bay of Gdansk from the Baltic Sea and created a large bay called the Bay of Puck. It was an ideal spot for water sports and leisure boating.

Our villa was one of a number scattered throughout a forest of pines.

The timber for the house came from that same forest, so the robust scent of pine from both inside the house and from the surrounding trees permeated our every breath.

Our garden was filled with roses; and there was a little pond surrounded with wild berries and heather. Majestic dunes and a wide beach of fine, pale-yellow sand were a short distance away. There were numerous jetties and shelters for small boats, which could be seen bobbing gently on the usually calm waters of the bay.

Our days usually consisted of mornings on the beach and afternoons either boating or playing games and sports. I have a particularly painful memory of one of those sporting events. It was a tennis match in which my opponent, who was stronger than I, wiped me out, as an audience of numerous friends watched. It was the first and last tournament of my life.

Most of my tennis playing prior to that time had been with André. We had spent many happy hours playing tennis at Garbow—this, in spite of some unique limitations to our tennis court. The landscape designer had been fiercely opposed to enclosing the court with a fence, saying it would disfigure the landscape. His solution was to plant a hedge of tall shrubs, as he believed that would stop the balls. It did more than that—it swallowed them. We had to go on regular searches for our tennis balls in a thicket of almost impenetrable hedge. Sometimes, we would enlist boys from the village to help us with our search. We also had to struggle with a dirt surface that lacked stability and that would change shape with each rain. In spite of these problems, we had great fun, and I even imagined our becoming champions—until one match at Jurata settled that.

Another match also lingers unhappily in my mind. Our father joined us one day for a game. All went well until I hit the ball very hard, and he lost control of his racket. It flew through the air, and the handle struck him on the cheek, which immediately became very swollen. I was mortified. My mother and a maid rushed to take care of his injury. That was the last time I played tennis with my father.

Swimming at Jurata meant venturing into the Baltic, which was usually around fourteen to sixteen degrees centigrade (fifty-seven to sixty degrees Fahrenheit). Children managed to have fun, but adults never ventured into the water. If the temperature dropped below fifty degrees Fahrenheit, I also chose to stay on shore.

Boating, however, was an unalloyed pleasure for us children. My father bought a Chris Craft motorboat, and it was high adventure for us to speed through the waves with the wind and water slapping at our faces. The Bay of Puck was generally very calm, but it could become dangerous during a storm. My parents took one boating trip when huge waves washed across the deck and began filling the Chris Craft. My mother, who didn't like water, had one of the worst frights of her life. Hours were spent in a harrowing struggle with rough seas. She said later that all she could think of the entire time was, "What will become of the children?"

A friend of our father, a Mr. Falter, had a faster and more impressive boat than ours. It was actually a luxurious yacht that could navigate the ocean. One day, Madame Falter invited our mother and us children for a little cruise on the Baltic. What should have been a pleasurable experience was marred by the fights I had with the other boy on board, whose snobbishness over their perceived superior class exasperated me. There was actually a great deal of such snobbishness at Jurata, which is not surprising, taking into account the number of wealthy people who vacationed there. One memorable incident occurred that demonstrated the artificiality and silliness of the lines between the classes. The Polish prime minister was among the prestigious visitors that summer, and he had his photo taken with our family. To the astonishment of most observers, the wife of our chauffeur, Budrys, was included in the photo. Unknown to all but our family, Budrys came from an old Lithuanian family, and his wife was the prime minister's sister.

In addition to being photographed with the prime minister, another incident occurred that summer to further elevate our family's social position in the artificial world of the wealthy elite. Our maternal grandparents had sold their historic estate, Stara Wies, to Prince Radziwill. The prince, a tall and elegant man, also visited Jurata that summer. One day, his heavy black Cadillac got stuck on a sandy road very close to our villa. With considerable difficulty, we helped his chauffeur extricate the car. In the evening, during the course of a reception in his honor, Prince Radziwill embraced my mother and then said to the gathering, "Madame Sophie and I have the same chariot." He was alluding to the carts (called *wuz* in Polish) used by peasants for transportation and carrying hay. Whether this was a reference to their connection through Stara Wies or that they both owned Cadillacs, it elevated even further my mother's social standing.

While we and most of the people we knew spent the summer of 1939 largely unconcerned about world events, the Polish government had begun to recognize the inevitability of a Nazi invasion. It ordered the repatriation of all capital placed in foreign investments in order to aid in the financing of the coming war effort. Our family held one of the largest fortunes in Poland. I remember hearing our father explain to our mother that "as good citizens," they should heed this order, so he withdrew all the money invested in London and Geneva. Unfortunately, it was already too late to save our country, as the war would be lost in a few weeks. His patriotism only succeeded in impoverishing our family.

Yet the confidence in the Polish forces was such that the rapid occupation of the country and the destruction of Warsaw seemed unthinkable. To my knowledge, my parents had made no arrangements to protect their precious objects—paintings, furniture, and other valuable possessions. They certainly were aware of the threat of war but, remembering World War I, they did not expect events to move swiftly. Until the last month before Poland was invaded, our father was quite absorbed in his business ventures, which were divided between shared family ventures and his own investments in industry and real estate. He continued to expand his holdings almost to the end. He invested in two buildings in a desirable quarter in Warsaw, and he bought land in Gdynia, a principal port town on the Baltic Sea. It was due for expansion, and he planned to construct a building there. He also bought Opalenica, the most important sugar factory in eastern Europe, which was situated on the German border. He would not have done this if he had any sense of what lay ahead, for it reduced the capital available for him to export from Poland in an emergency. It also provoked the displeasure of the long-time German stockholders and the attempt by the Gestapo to try to find my father after Poland was defeated.

During what were to be our last days in Poland, our mother was with us in Garbow, while our father was occupied with business in Warsaw. As the end of August approached, it was becoming clear to many that war was imminent. Polish troops, mobilized in great haste, were deploying the length of the German frontier. The radio was full of martial airs, as well as songs that ridiculed Hitler. I still recall the beginning of a song: *Hitler palcem rusza w bucie a my sobie gwizdzem na to* ("Hitler moves his finger in his boot, but we don't care").

How could we have been so unaware? As August came to an end, we were serenely confident of our place in the world. One day later, our lives changed forever.

Le blason de la famille BRONIEWSKI

Le blason "herb" TARNAWA

Le blason a été créé pour honorer les chevaliers qui se sont distingués lors de la bataille de TARNAWA, nom du massif montagneux, théâtre des hostillités. Le roi de Pologne, Boleslaw II, a rendu officiel le blason en l'an 1068.

D'après les chroniques de l'époque, en 1728, dix sept familles, incluant les BRONIEWSKI, avaient droit au blason TARNAWA.

Coat of Arms Tarnawa

Herb Lis z odmianą Bzura
przysługujący rodzinie JERLICZ,
GERLICZ.

Coat of Arms Gerlicz

Portrait of a forbear, possibly the author's great-great-grandfather, from around the beginning of the nineteenth century, showing the Tarnawa coat of arms attributed to the Broniewski family

Bogdan's maternal grandfather, Aleksander Gerlicz (1868–1934), painted in 1930 by famous Polish artist Zofia Rudzkah

Bronislaw Broniewski, author's great-grandfather (1825–1875?), painted by his son Kazimierz

Bogdan's father, Mieczyslaw Broniewski (1893–1966), painted in 1938 by famous Polish portrait artist Barbacki, who was executed by the Gestapo

Bogdan's mother, Zofia Broniewska (1892–1978), painted in 1939 by world-famous artist Czedekowski

LWÓW *Maria* KRYNICA

Eugenie Broniewska, author's grandmother, born in Vienna in 1865

Author's grandparents, Bohdan and Eugenie, circa 1883 (at ages 27 and 19)

Eugenie with daughter Christine, Bogdan's aunt

Author's great-grandmother, Ewa Koszutska, circa 1900

Author's grandparents—Grandfather Gerlicz had his leg amputated

Aleksander Gerlicz, far left in back seat, in his Phaeton convertible, 1928

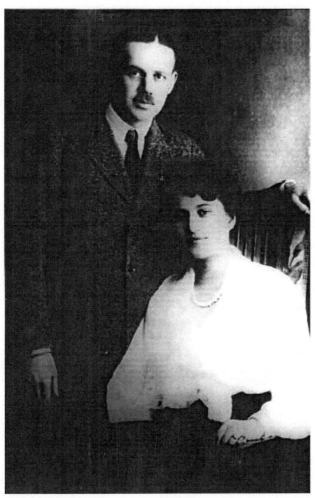

Author's uncle and aunt, Zygmunt and Stephanie, ages 40 and 28, in 1930

Front row from left: Eugenie, Christine, Ewa Koszutska; second row from left: author's father, Mieczyslaw, grandfather Bohdan, a tutor, Zygmunt, an uncle, and a second tutor

Bogdan Broniewski, two years old—Garbow, 1924

André and the author, Bogdan—Garbow, 1927

Bogdan and André at ages 10 and 9

A bryczka on edge of forest at Garbow

Workers' children at Przybyslawice, Garbow

Bogdan and Marysia distributing presents to workers' children

Children's camp created by author's father at Przybyslawice

Author's mother and father, Mieczyslaw and Zofia, Warsaw, circa 1935–1936

Gerlicz family coat of arms above door at Stara Wies

Stara Wies doorway

Stara Wies, where author's mother spent her early years

View of Stara Wies

Morning exercises, from left: André, Marysia, and author, Bogdan

Author's father after killing stag

Warsaw residence, No. 25 Mokotowska, circa 1937

Author's father in front of Warsaw residence, 1936

Painting by Jan Styka (Eunice with Petroniusz) that hung in entry hall of Warsaw residence

Early photo of Garbow residence, Pryzybyslawice

Later photo of Garbow residence

Marysia driving her pony cart

Marysia in park at Pryzybyslawice

.CZTERY WIDOKI PRZYBYSŁAWIC
/DWOR, PERGOLA I ALTANKA/
WYKONANE PRZEZ PROFESORA STA-
NISŁAWA NIEWIADOMSKIEGO w 1939=

Drawings of Przybyslawice in late 1930s

Author's sister, Marysia, 1932

A maid and fat cook at Zakopane in Tatra Mountains, 1937

Bogdan and his mother, Zofia, at Zakopane

Goral in Zakopane Mountains

André, Marysia, and mother, Zofia, at Zakopane

Marysia and one of her many dolls

Arbor at Przybyslawice

André's hunting companion, Le Grand Duc

André with birds he shot

Book Two

Peril

Chapter 16
Flight

URING THE EARLY HOURS on the morning of September 4, we took to the road from Garbow, heading for Zaleszczyki on the edge of the river Dniestr. Romania lay on the other side of the river. We were accompanied by a veritable convoy of cars that contained friends fleeing Warsaw who had briefly sought refuge with us at Garbow. Before leaving, we bid farewell to Stephanie and Zygmunt. Nothing cut so to my heart as that farewell. I had a presentiment that I was saying good-bye forever. It was indeed the last time that I would see my aunt.

Our flight from the approaching enemy must have been one of the grander and more singular of such exercises. Unlike the heart-wrenching war films showing lines of refugees fleeing on foot, pushing all their belongings before them in a variety of carts and conveyances, we fled in two large Cadillacs. Our entourage included our parents, André and me, Marysia, our English governess, and our luggage. We also had a chauffeur to drive one of the cars. He was actually our father's valet, substituting for Budrys, who had been mobilized into the Polish military. Our father had a driving accident in his youth in which a passenger had been thrown from the car, and he never wished to drive again, so André and I were to take turns driving the second car.

The convoy took the main road that connected Warsaw to southeast

Poland. We traveled through Lublin, the county seat of the region, and then the medieval city of Zamose, and then Lwow, before reaching our destination of Zaleszczyki. We traveled a well-maintained and generally satisfactory road, but several days of heavy traffic had caused deep holes in the road, and driving became difficult, even dangerous. Yet the much greater danger was the air raids by the Luftwaffe—the city of Lwow was bombed just days before we passed through. Thus, it took two days to reach our destination. It was a harrowing two days as we listened and watched for German planes overhead, while trying to avoid crippling holes in the torn-up road.

Cars of that period were not equipped with radios, so during our two days of travel we were completely cut off from the news, which greatly added to our stress. On arriving at Zaleszczyki, we finally were able to get hold of the latest military information and could measure the extent of the disaster. It was alarming. The German troops had already invaded Warsaw and were occupying a major part of the country. The same Hermann Goering, Master of the German Hunt and of the German Forests, who spared the forest of Bialowieza because he often hunted there, also commanded the German air force that conducted the blitzkrieg that smashed Polish resistance.

We stayed at Zaleszczyki for several days while our parents made preparations for the next part of the trip. Although fleeing for our lives, we were expected to go through customs formalities. However our parents, though experiencing the crushing weight of events, did not include us children in their acutely critical decisions, so André and I were able to briefly ignore the enormity of our situation and pretend we were tourists.

The picturesque village of Zaleszczyki was filled with historical sites. Its ideal climate made it a popular health resort. It was situated between a peninsula at the mouth of the Dniestr River and the base of the Carpatians, the massive mountains in southern Poland, where our father once spent several cold nights waiting to kill a bear.

The Zaleszczyki lands had belonged to the Poniatowski family. Prince Josephe Poniatowski, a very popular figure in Poland, was the nephew of King Stanislas Poniatowski. He created a large park at Zaleszczyki and a garden theatre that was well known in the region. In Warsaw, one can still see a Renaissance-style palace with a roof covered with copper tiles. It was an official residence of Prince Poniatowski and is well known by Poles as *palac pod blacha*. In 1813, Josephe Poniatowski, who commanded the Polish units of the Grand Napoleon Army, perished while crossing the River Elster in Russia, during the retreat of the Grand Army.

On the other side of the Dniestr extended a foreign country, Romania, where we would soon venture. Refugees from all over were arriving in our hotel and preparing to cross the border. Upon the receipt of alarming news that the Soviets might be invading from the east, our father decided to leave Poland quickly. In addition to obtaining Romanian visas, it was also necessary to stock up on gasoline. That was not an easy task; gas was lacking in both Poland and Romania. It was approximately six hundred miles to Bucharest. Thus, it was necessary to take into account both the distance and the substantial fuel consumption of two large, heavy cars. Once the obstacles to obtaining the gas were overcome, there was the problem of how to store and transport it. There were no metal jerricans (a five-gallon container for carrying fluids) to be found. The only option was to carry the extra gas in two large glass demijohns (also for carrying fluids of up to 10 gallons)—a highly treacherous way to carry gasoline.

Early on the morning of September 12, all was ready for us to leave Poland. Our father's valet and impromptu chauffeur had to leave us at the border. He was to be married to Francoise, who most recently had been our mother's maid. (When we were little, she had been André's governess.) This was another sad parting. Francoise had refused to leave our home in Warsaw. It was her home also. All her family—her sisters, their husbands, and other family members— had worked for us for at least two generations. She was very attached to us and saw our troubles as her own. But she couldn't imagine fleeing with us. She would stay put and wait for our return.

We later learned that she was killed during a bombing raid and was buried in the little garden at our Warsaw home. At the end of the war, with the capital in ruins, Warsaw was strewn with hundreds of thousands of little crosses, showing where people had been buried. Years later, their bodies were exhumed and buried in a little cemetery created for this purpose. That is where Francoise lies. She had been a fierce and courageous defender of our home and possessions, hoping that we would eventually rejoin her in Warsaw. That was not to be. Indeed, nothing was ever to be the same. Events were swiftly severing us from everything familiar and propelling us forward into a life we couldn't even imagine.

We started the next lap of our journey with André driving the car in which my parents and Marysia rode, while I drove the car with the English governess, the luggage, and the demijohns full of gas. This was a curious division of responsibilities, for I was a rather nervous, erratic driver. Perhaps my father felt more comfortable being driven by André, but considering the quantity of gasoline and the fragility of the glass demijohns, my car was in danger of exploding at the slightest mishap. Although I was aware of this, our English governess, happily, was not.

We crossed the border and traversed the bridge on the Dniestr without major difficulties, in spite of the number of refugees who were hurrying to flee Poland. Luck was with us, for several days later, on September 17, the Soviets, following a secret agreement they had with Germany, invaded from the east. The border with the Soviet Union was around fifty kilometers from Zaleszczyki, and the Soviet tanks would be able to reach the city at any moment, sealing off the border and preventing access to Romania. When this news struck, hundreds of vehicles of all kinds stormed the bridge on the Dniestr. It was a scene of panic—how could so many pass over the bridge? How many would arrive too late? I never knew.

Some years later, we were to learn of another attempt to flee that occurred at about the same time. Important detachments of the Polish army had been withdrawing toward the east, hoping to take advantage of the Prypec marshes as a natural line of defense. But they clashed with the Red Army troops who were just penetrating Poland, in order to reach the line of demarcation that had been fixed in the secret accord between Hitler and Stalin. Caught in a vise between the Germans and the Soviets, numerous elements of the Polish army had to surrender to the Red Army. This presented Stalin with the opportunity to decapitate the Polish elite, which then constituted a serious force that was able to oppose the Communist regime and Soviet domination. In the following months, the Soviets executed thousands of Polish officers who had been taken as prisoners of war. A simple means was a bullet in the back of the neck and then mass burial in an inaccessible place; the Katyn Forest near Smolensk met this requirement. Discovery of the mass grave in the Katyn Forest in

April 1943 led to charges and counter-charges between the Soviets and the Nazis and a less-than-satisfactory response from Poland's allies, who were focused on their own strategic concerns. The incident is recorded in history books as the "Katyn Massacre."

Chapter 17

On to Bucharest

BUCHAREST IS IN SOUTHERN Romania, near the border with Bulgaria. In order to get there, we had to traverse almost the entire country, traveling from north to south along the eastern base of the Carpathian Mountains. Driving with my dangerous cargo kept me almost fully absorbed, leaving me with only fragmentary memories of the trip. I couldn't help noticing, however, how poor the country seemed in comparison to Poland. Electrical poles of raw, untreated timber stood askew along the sides of poorly maintained roads—roads that were clogged with a motley assemblage of cars of all ages, makes, and conditions that were, filled with refugees, fleeing, just as we were. I felt awkwardly conspicuous in our two-car caravan of large, late-model Cadillacs.

It took two arduous, nerve-jarring days to make the trip. Just as we approached the outskirts of Bucharest, an enormous dog appeared suddenly in front of my car. I was afraid to brake forcefully because of the demijohns full of gasoline. I tried swerving sharply, but couldn't avoid hitting the dog. I pulled to the side of the road to see if there was anything I could do. As I got out of the car, the dog stood up to its full height, let out a terrible howl, and fell dead right before me. I stood there, feeling as if some action was required on my part but could think of nothing to do. My father stepped out of his car and put his arm around my shoulder, "Come, Danek," he said, using my pet name, "we have to keep going." I got back into my car feeling shaken, and I drove off leaving what was the first—and I hoped the last—fatal victim of my driving lying in the middle of the road. My passenger, the governess, tried to restore a sense of calm by repeating several times that I was a "good boy" and that it was all "that big dog's fault."

When we reached Bucharest, we found lodgings in a palace that had been converted to a hotel. It was full of Polish refugees. I don't know where other refugees stayed, but our hotel housed diplomats, prominent politicians, army officers, and well-to-do families. Our governess left us at that point to try to make her way back to England. Like so many partings in wartime, there was the unspoken knowledge of finality and an uncertain outcome. But we spoke only words of encouragement and false cheer, as our lives turned irrevocably in different directions.

This was my first trip to a foreign country, and I began to feel disoriented. I also became aware of a possibility too big to fully comprehend—that perhaps we had left our country forever. Very soon it became apparent that I was not the only one with such feelings. Everywhere I turned in the hotel, groups of compatriots were gathered in little clusters, with discussions going full force. The subject was always the same—an uneasy sense of dislocation, of anguish over the future of our country, and a profound awareness of an uncertain destiny awaiting each of us.

My father was weathering this crisis in relatively good form. He had decided that we would stay only a few days in Bucharest, just long enough to accomplish several formalities (i.e., obtain visas for France—the destination our parents had chosen—and organize the rest of our trip). The first thing he did was sell our two cars—at a price that I thought was appallingly low. With the money from the transaction, he paid the hotel bill and bought first-class tickets on the sleeping cars of the Orient Express. Next, he took André, Marysia, and me shopping for new clothes and linens. My mother was horrified when she saw the extent of our purchases. "Now that we are becoming poor, how can you waste money like this?" My father responded, "We have to spend it here in Romania. It will be worth nothing in France." Thus, we started the last lap of our journey in great splendor. We boarded the Orient Express wearing elegant new clothes and carrying fine, new suitcases that held the rest of our purchases.

Chapter 18

Destination Paris

THE ORIENT EXPRESS TRAVELED once or twice a week between Ankara, Turkey, and Paris. It traversed a large part of Europe, crossing from east to west through Bulgaria, Romania, Austria, Yugoslavia, Italy, and Switzerland, before arriving in France. For first-class passengers like us, every possible comfort and convenience was provided. We had two connecting compartments—one for my parents and Marysia, and one for André and me. Comfortable beds were prepared for us at nighttime, and breakfast was brought to our compartments each morning. We took the rest of our meals in the elegant dining car. To the best of my memory, the trip took two days and two nights.

A number of diplomats who were fleeing Poland were on the train with us, including the American ambassador to Poland, Drexell Biddle, and the French ambassador, a Monsieur Noel. The latter did not know what awaited him upon his return to his country, for France and England had declared war on Germany as soon as Poland was invaded. The American ambassador, however, knew no such concerns. His casual, light-hearted demeanor stood in jarring contrast to the somber demeanor of his French counterpart. It would be two years before the United States would be drawn into the conflict that was roiling much of Europe.

Ambassador Biddle had been a prominent figure in Poland,

where my parents had occasion to know him. It was interesting to observe someone of his stature. He paid a visit to my parents in their compartment and ate in the dining car at the same time as our family did. He was an athletic, distinguished-looking man, who wore the mantle of privilege and power with great ease. His wife, wearing white makeup, seemed a veritable ghost, and their son, who was accompanied by a pretty girlfriend, appeared to be a typical playboy.

We had not yet begun to recognize the large gap that was opening between us and people of Ambassador Biddle's social standing. For him, the Polish tragedy signified only a change of careers. For us, it would mean the loss of everything: our country, our possessions, and our wealth.

The trip on the Orient Express was full of many such contradictions. We were traveling in luxury while having suffered financial ruin. We were anticipating arriving in the dazzling city of Paris, while coping with the abrupt and possibly permanent separation from our native soil. We were charmed by the momentary beauty outside the train windows, while struggling with anxiety over what awaited us at the end of our journey.

I remember particularly a stunning view of Lac Leman against the Swiss Alps. I gazed out the window and wished that we could stop in that beautiful country. Little could I have guessed that many years later, and in what would seem several lifetimes away, I would actually return to that spot.

As we neared the end of our journey, I was overcome by a mixture of excitement and dread. Never in my life had I felt such lack of control. It was as if events had seized me in an unshakeable grip and were propelling me forward. The train reached its destination, and I stepped off, with no idea of what would happen next. I just kept following our parents' lead as events unfolded, literally, minute by minute.

Upon our arrival in Paris, I couldn't help but notice that Ambassador Biddle was greeted by a delegation and left in a large limousine, while the French ambassador took a taxi, like everyone else. For us, the excitement of arriving in Paris—the capital of the world—allowed us to temporarily forget that we were cut adrift from anything that gave us a sense of permanence and place. The first euphoria of being in Paris also allowed us to forget, for just a little bit longer, that we had become relatively poor. Soon enough, we would face that reality, along with another truth equally as profound—that although the separation from the life we had known could be measured in miles and weeks, it was to be beyond measure in the changes wrought.

We stayed briefly in a deluxe hotel in the Champs-Elysées, a place my father had known before the war. Soon, however, an ever-growing unease over our precarious situation caused us to move to more modest lodgings. A little hotel, which still exists today, the Madison Elysee, situated on rue Galilee, sheltered us for the next several weeks.

Those few weeks were a heady interlude for André and me. Our parents were too preoccupied to pay much attention to us. We spent our days wandering free, like anonymous visitors from another planet, through the most beautiful quarters of Paris, including the Etoile, the Champs-Elysées, the Trocadero, and the Place de la Concorde. It was an exhilarating, sudden immersion into the wonders of one of the world's greatest cities. But our exhilaration was soon tempered by the news coming from Poland.

Chapter 19

Poland Is Lost

BY THE TIME WE arrived in Paris, Poland's fate was sealed. From the first day of the offensive, Hitler's armored troops had cut through the Polish defense and occupied the country up to the demarcation line agreed upon with the Soviets before the invasion. The juncture of this line was reached by September 18, and Hitler announced Germany's victory over Poland.

In reality, the fighting did not stop on that date. There were still scattered pockets of resistance, especially in Warsaw. It was under attack from the first day of hostilities but refused to surrender. The heroic defense of Warsaw aroused the emotions and admiration of the entire world, but little was done to help. The Luftwaffe was daily dropping hundreds of incendiary bombs, and flames lay siege to the city. At the end of approximately one month of resistance, the munitions and supplies were exhausted, the communication lines cut, and water pipes and electric cables destroyed. The loss of human life was enormous. The defenders of Warsaw, and those who survived the relentless assault, had to surrender. Warsaw lay in ruins.

Soon the length of the main residential avenue of Warsaw, *Aleje Ujazdowskie*, became a parade ground, as Hitler watched his triumphant troops march past. The remaining residents were ordered to stay in their houses and close their shutters, under threat of being shot on the spot. This parade was the forerunner for another event, even grander, which would take place ten months later. Then the setting would be the Champs-Elysées in Paris.

During the weeks that followed the news from Poland, I was tortured with thoughts of my country's defeat and our inability to get any information about the loved ones we had left behind. I wanted desperately to be an active participant, instead of a helpless and distant observer. I kept imagining myself as a heroic general fighting off the German invasion. Years later, I would study many historical documents devoted to World War II. At age seventeen, I wrote my own report. It was an unpretentious document, written on a school notebook in an adolescent hand. It is the sole document I have preserved from my experience of being present at one of history's great epics; it has been with me for over sixty years. Even though it is written in Polish—*Kampana w Polsce* (Polish Campaign), I have attached it as an appendix to this memoir.

While we were preoccupied with the news about Poland, discussions were already underway for the establishment of a provisional Polish government in France. Headquarters were soon established just three hundred kilometers southwest of Paris at Angers in the Loire Valley. The first president was the celebrated pianist Jan Paderewski. The main priority of this fledgling government-in-exile was to organize the overseas struggle against the German oppressors. My father participated in the preliminary work but declined the opportunity to be part of the operation. He didn't like many of the politicians and doubted whether they could be effective. Thus, another tie to our homeland was severed.

Chapter 20

A Difficult Passage

ONCE IT WAS DECIDED not to go to Angers to participate in the government-in-exile, my parents looked for lodging less temporary than the hotel we were in at the time. They rented an apartment situated on Boulevard St. Germain, in the Latin Quarter of Paris.

Until that time we had lived in hotels with housekeepers to maintain our rooms, and we ate our meals in small nearby restaurants. The move to an apartment opened a miserable new chapter for my mother, who had never kept house or cooked. It seemed as though she spent much of her time crying. It was a struggle to master just the basic skills to put a meal on the table. While her husband dealt with the outside world, and her children were either in school or heedlessly pursuing their own interests, she was grappling with her newfound domestic responsibilities. Two attempts were made to provide some help but neither of the hired women lasted. They both had irascible dispositions and both departed abruptly, leaving my mother again in tears.

I particularly remember one meal. After we all had been determinedly sawing at a mysterious cut of meat for several minutes, we had to admit defeat. It was impossible to cut. André even picked it up in his hands and tried gnawing at it, but with no better results. The vegetables were equally daunting. The large carrot on my plate had apparently spent only enough time in the pot to change its temperature.

It was essentially a raw, hot carrot. The potatoes and cabbage had gone in the other direction and were soggy and slightly burned. After my mother's weeping declaration, "I'll never learn how to cook," our somber little band headed for a familiar restaurant.

Gradually, a few small, bright spots emerged among the gloom. A laundry close by, run by a Polish count who also was struggling to adapt to his refugee status, provided my mother with some friendly exchanges with someone of a shared culture. Then we discovered a Polish restaurant, where we ate occasionally. The best contact of all was a distinguished Polish woman who held a salon in the evenings for her fellow countrymen. My mother attended whenever she could. Both of my parents spoke excellent French, particularly my mother, who had been educated in an exclusive girls school in Switzerland. This was an enormous help in making the extremely difficult adjustment to her drastically altered circumstances.

My memory of my father during that period is that he was ill-tempered most of the time. Where once we lived our lives separated by the customs and accommodations of extreme wealth, we were now compressed into a physical space so small that only our parents and sister had bedrooms. I slept in the small living room, and André slept in the hallway. Cataclysmic events had drawn us closer together but in a physical sense only. They did not bring about an emotional intimacy. In fact, I tried to avoid my father as much as possible. I began to stutter again and was often sick with colds and sore throats. If this caused me to stay home, my father would exclaim, "*Est-ce que la grippe est une maladie?*" (Is a cold a malady?)

My relationship with André was not harmonious either. It seemed as though much of our time together was spent arguing about what was happening in Poland. He felt that Poland could have provided better resistance to the Nazis, and I argued that Poland was incapable of winning for two fundamental reasons—the inequality of the forces, both in quantity and quality; and the length of the border with Germany that lacked any natural obstacles.

The Germans had sixty divisions armed with powerful guns, unknown until then. Several of the divisions were armored units equipped with heavy tanks. At total, more than two million men were engaged in the operations. On the Polish side, the army had thirty divisions, of which the majority had only light equipment—principally cavalry brigades—and no armored units, for a total of around a half-million men. The German army was equipped with four thousand planes of top quality, the majority of which were bombers. Poland had only four hundred airplanes, and they were of inferior quality. Thus, the Luftwaffe controlled the Polish skies from the first day of the war.

The length of the border with Germany extended 1,500 kilometers, with few natural obstacles. In fact, the topography of Poland, except for the mountains in the south, consists of large plains that form part of a geological structure characteristic of central Europe.

I felt that many lives and much suffering could possibly have been spared if the politicians and the Polish military had recognized these realities before the beginning of the hostilities. It was a source of great annoyance to me that I couldn't even convince André of the hopelessness of Poland's struggle.

My favorite escape from family friction was the many hours I spent wandering among the bookstores in the Latin Quarter. However, the time for such leisurely pursuits narrowed down considerably as October and the beginning of a new school year arrived.

In spite of our precarious foothold in a foreign culture, and with the threat of another invasion looming over us, it was necessary to think about our schooling. It was then that our father made a major decision that affected his children's future. Most of our young compatriots who arrived in France chose to attend a Polish school. Our father decided, instead, to enroll us in a French school. It was a decision for which I remain forever grateful. I remember his saying, "We don't know if we will ever be able to return to our country. You need to prepare yourselves to stay in France and earn your living here." His decision was not only wise, but it also perhaps saved our lives.

When the Germans would eventually invade France, the Polish high school moved to Grenoble, which was a veritable nest of resistance against the German occupation. The Polish students were swept up, in one fashion or another, with the Resistance. Grenoble was close to the Alps, which offered effective protection for the Maquisard, a name given to Resistance fighters living in the Maquis. It was an arid and savage region that favored the exploits of commandos. Of particular importance was the Massif of Vercors. Its high plateau offered perfect protection. It could only be accessed by narrow, somewhat steep roads, which were impracticable for the German army's heavy equipment.

It was used by the Resistance for assembling troops and performing military exercises, but it was not adequate for landing airplanes.

When the fortunes of war began to turn against the Germans, the subversive actions of the Maquis became intolerable to them. One night, they blocked all access to the Massif of Vercors with powerful military detachments, thus isolating the entire Massif and the Maquisards who were operating there. At sunrise a squadron of gliders, full of heavily armed special troops, landed on the plateau. The Maquisards were taken by surprise. It was carnage! The Germans took no prisoners— they killed everyone on the plateau and on the exit roads from the Massif. No one was able to escape. But for our father's decision, André and I might have been among the dead.

Chapter 21

Back to School

DURING OUR FIRST MONTHS in Paris, the massacre at Vercors still lay ahead. As fragile and rootless transplants in unfamiliar soil, we were still sorting out, from day to day, how we were to live.

Soon it became time to select a school, and we had no idea how to proceed. Just by chance, while walking on the Boulevard Saint Michel, not far from our apartment, I noticed a large high school. It was the Lycee Saint Louis. Despite some difficulties, my father succeeded in enrolling André and me. He had no way of knowing if he was making a good choice, but it turned out that we were in the very best French high school for the sciences. Each year, a majority of its students passed the competitive entry examination for the top schools, notably l'Ecole Polytechnique.

We found ourselves thrust into a merciless system where, at each of four successive levels, those students who couldn't meet the school's high standards were weeded out. The final level, which lasted two years, was so difficult that traditionally, half of the students were obliged to drop out. Those who stayed had one foot in the Ecole Polytechnique. The students of this prestigious school were able to hope for brilliant careers in either the government or the public sector.

I soon began to imagine myself as ascending to the grandest heights. I was confident that I was gifted in math, and I could see myself scaling the pyramid of exams and arriving triumphantly at the summit. I was a little like the foolish milkmaid in the children's fairy tale, *Pierrette et le pot au lait,* who plans all the things she is going to buy when she sells the pot of milk she is carrying on her head. Like the foolish milkmaid, all my hopes were dashed as my pot fell and broke, and the milk spilled out on the ground. The director of the school sent a letter to my father, summoning him to a meeting. He was told, "Unfortunately, your sons are not sufficiently advanced to follow the course, particularly in French, where they can't make the distinction between two simple little words, pronounced quite differently and with very different meanings: *et* and *est.*"

Those many tedious hours spent studying French with our governess in Poland had served me well to that point. From the moment of our arrival in France, I had been able to understand and respond to much of what we heard. Now, I was paying a price for my stubborn refusal to master French grammar and spelling.

We really weren't prepared, however, to pass the *baccalaureate,* the compulsory test for advancement to the next level in the rigid French educational system. Our father was asked to take us out of the school. He was stricken, but I considered myself capable of succeeding, and I set out to prove the director wrong.

At this point, our family again changed its residence in Paris to rue Singer, a small, quiet residential street in Passy. I never really knew the state of our finances. Our father did not reveal many details of what he was able to take with him when we fled Poland. We did know, however, that our circumstances were drastically changed, and money was now a consideration in our choices of where and how to live.

We were soon enrolled in St. Jean de Passy, a private high school in our new neighborhood. Perhaps because it was a private school with paying students, it housed a considerable number of dunces and rich kids (these terms were sometimes interchangeable). Here, life was easy, and I found myself making friends for the first time. It was the very opposite of the austere and competitive Lycee Saint Louis. In this atmosphere, I was almost straightaway elevated to first place in math. Not satisfied to rest on my laurels, I bought a booklet that had the problems in math and physics that had been submitted to the candidates to the baccalaureate in previous years. I applied myself assiduously to studying and solving every one of the problems. After several months of intense study, I passed the baccalaureate with ease—just before our attention was again turned to the war.

Chapter 22

The German Juggernaut

W HEN WE ARRIVED IN Paris at the end of September 1939, France and England had been officially at war with Nazi Germany for several weeks. They were honoring, in word if not in deed, the tripartite agreement signed with Poland several months before. In spite of their declaration of war against Germany, nothing seemed to be happening. The front with Germany would remain one of total calm until the devastating offensive of the Wehrmacht in the coming spring. This period became known as *une drole de guerre,* or "the phony war." It was a period of such ennui for the waiting soldiers at the ill-fated Maginot Line that they were sent flowers so they could occupy themselves with planting and growing gardens.

All was not as it seemed, however. In fact, both the Germans and the Allies were involved in intense preparation for the coming conflict. A French and British integrated command was created, with General Maurice Gamelin as head of the *etat major.* British ships were offloading military materiel in France, along with the hundreds of thousands of men that were needed to supplement the French fighting forces. The Nazis were reinforcing their armies, increasing the production of armaments, and putting the final details in place for an invasion that would quickly pulverize the French and British defense.

During the months when I was preoccupied with my studies, the Germans had been concentrating their efforts and resources on their war machine. They were amassing overwhelming forces on the Western Front—enough armored divisions and a sufficient air force to paralyze the enemy. The superiority of the Germans was measured not only by the size and strength of its armaments but also by the psychological factor. Hitler's messianic fanaticism had succeeded in mobilizing much of the German population behind his crusade to conquer much of Europe.

In contrast France, which wanted with all its heart to avoid war, was ill-prepared for the coming conflict. French forces didn't compare in quantity or quality to the Nazi forces. As for the British, their ground forces were not much better than those of the French. Their navy, however, continued to dominate the seas, which helped avoid a total disaster when the Western Front collapsed. Clearly, the coordination of the leadership of troops from two different countries was extremely difficult, and even worse, it was defective at the summit, where the general in charge was in question.

The unstable regime in France had waited until the last moment before the launching of the German offensive to act. Paul Reynaud succeeded Edouard Daladier in March as the premier (*President du Conseil*). Reynaud, believing General Gamelin unequal to the task at hand, demanded his replacement. But the general had political support, and his removal was refused. As a consequence, Paul Reynaud submitted his resignation. Unfortunately, it was not effectuated because all efforts were focused on preparation for the imminent German offensive. This meant that at a critical moment, France was technically without a government, and its armies were commanded by a general who did not seem to be up to the overwhelming task ahead.

Additionally, the French put their major focus on the Maginot Line, the heavily fortified barricade on the northeastern border between France and Germany. It was certainly the most elaborate barricade ever built—it had thicker concrete than had ever been used before. There were underground rail lines, living quarters, garages, storehouses, hospitals, even recreation areas. But it proved to be virtually useless. When the invasion would come, the Germans would circumvent the Line by going through Belgium.

On April 9, 1940, Germany sent an ultimatum to Denmark and Norway. Denmark capitulated, but Norway tried to defend itself. In spite of the fierce resistance around the large ports of the North Sea—

Oslo, Trondheim, Narvik—the German troops occupied the central nerve center of the country the same day. The occupation of Denmark and Norway gave the Nazis strategic positions for controlling the North Sea in future operations.

Events began to move swiftly. On May 10, German troops invaded Holland and Belgium, using the pretext that it was done for their protection. The two countries soon capitulated. The grand offensive against France began at dawn the next day.

I recall a particularly pathetic speech one evening by Prime Minister Reynaud, telling of a large breach in the French line that the Wehrmacht opened on the very first day of combat. Following tactics already used in Poland, the German armored divisions had pierced the French and British defenses. The breach opened into a gaping hole on the second day, enabling the superior German armored divisions to rush through. The objective was to isolate the Maginot Line and encircle the troops, mostly British, who were defending the north sector of the front.

For those of us who had lived through the Polish campaign, the outcome of the ensuing battles on French soil was tragically clear. Even though the shorter frontiers and mountains made the French terrain more suitable for defense than the long, flat frontiers of Poland, nothing could stop the German juggernaut. The Maginot Line only served to prolong military operations and cause the French to have a foolish complacence about their invulnerability. The final result was preordained. Faced with the superiority of the German forces, resistance became impossible, and the high British command decided on the evacuation of their troops. What followed was one of the most remarkable and successful military movements in history. The British pressed every available craft into service, including yachts and trawlers operated largely by amateur seamen. Between May 23 and May 27, more than five thousand troops were evacuated from the ports of Boulogne and Calais. The last to be evacuated from Calais were taken out at night. Soon, the advance of German tanks and the surrender of the Belgians, which exposed an important section of the front line, left Dunkirk as the only escape route. But the Luftwaffe bombing put the harbor out of use, and the thousands yet to be evacuated were ferried out to waiting destroyers by small craft, including fishing boats and rowboats. By June 4, when the withdrawal ended, around 198,000 British and 140,000 French and Belgian troops were saved.

Why Hitler ordered his troops to stop, instead of rushing Dunkirk to prevent the evacuation, is one of the great enigmas of the Second World War. The simplest answer is that even great military strategists make mistakes, and Hitler would go on to make other fatal blunders.

It is also impossible to know what the reaction of the English people would have been if hundreds of thousands of British soldiers had been taken prisoner or killed by the Nazis. It is probable that the history of the war would have been quite different.

The rapid escalation of the German offensive was frightening to the French. For us, it foretold impending catastrophe. Poland's experience had removed all illusions. In our apartment in Passy, we listened to the radio every evening. Our uneasiness increased with each piece of alarming news. It was not necessary for us to wait to see the Nazis at the Paris gates. We knew it was only a question of days—or at the most, weeks. We made plans to leave Paris as quickly as possible.

Chapter 23

Our Flight Resumes

I RETURNED TO MY SCHOOL, St. Jean de Passy, to take leave of my teachers and friends. They were very surprised that we had decided to desert the capital. I remember one of my friends saying confidently, "Paris will not be taken." He expressed the general feeling held by many. It would be less than a month before they would be proven wrong.

But where were we to go? My father opened a map of France and put his finger on the city of Toulouse. It appeared to be an important city in southwestern France. With little time to waste, we chose that as our immediate destination. We could decide what to do next, once we got there.

The train to Toulouse was full of refugees from Belgium, Holland, and Luxembourg who had fled the Nazi occupation of their countries. Now, they were insane with worry, as they were fleeing again. At one station I saw a mother crying after she had become separated from her son; she ran the length of the train, searching for him. By contrast, there were very few French leaving. They didn't join the exodus until about ten days later.

When we reached Toulouse, the main hotel was already full. The sympathetic proprietor installed us in a little room that was used as a living room. Any lingering sense we had of being prosperous expatriates vanished as we made do with our little room and confronted our precarious situation as refugees.

My father now was considering that we should leave France entirely. The next day, he went to the Spanish consulate to obtain travel visas, but he gave up when he saw the large crowd of people there before him with the same idea. Like so many decisions made that are governed by the immediate circumstances at hand, this decision would have a profound and lasting effect on the course of our lives. As we took stock of our situation, it became clear that the only way we could get out of the country was by car. We bought a used 301 Peugeot, a small, dependable car with low gas consumption—a feature that was very important, for it would become increasingly difficult to buy fuel. However, it immediately became evident that our 301 was not designed to carry five people and all their luggage. My parents and sister arranged themselves as best they could in a backseat meant for just two people; André and I, who took turns driving, occupied the front seats. We put what luggage we could fit into the car's trunk and, on the advice of the garage owner, we bought a roof rack.

With our suitcases loaded on top of the car, we took off toward Spain. We had gone only a short way when suitcases began bouncing off of the car's roof and onto the hood. Sometimes they would come to rest directly in front of the windshield, blocking our view of the road, and other times they would slide off onto the ground. With each new jolt we would skid to the side of the road, get out, and try to safely secure the suitcases to the luggage rack. It was an intolerable situation that would have been comic if it hadn't been so dangerous for we were traveling narrow, sinuous roads. With everyone's nerves frayed and our forward progress severely impeded by suitcases bouncing on and off the car's hood, I became desperate to do something. Finally, with a bit of study and experimentation, I figured out how the luggage rack was supposed to work, and we took off toward the city of Pau, with passengers and suitcases both snug and secure. Our overloaded car looked like a slightly affluent version of the Joads' in *The Grapes of Wrath*.

When we arrived in Pau, we were one step closer to Spain. As in Toulouse, we found a pleasant hotel that, in spite of being crowded, was able to accommodate us. Pau, an ancient and picturesque city, was just fifty kilometers from the Pyrenees. The panoramic view of those mountains as we drove on the main boulevard was spectacular. In spite of the gravity of unfolding events, we found ourselves captivated by the beauty and grandeur of our surroundings.

Ours was a bifurcated journey. We were part refugees and part tourists. Thus, it was decided that we would find some beautiful spot in the Pyrenees to rest and temporarily try to forget our perilous situation. On the advice of hotel employees, we headed for Cauterets, a charming village situated in a valley surrounded by high mountains. We rented a little house there for several days. It was late spring, an especially beautiful time of the year. The mountains were still snow-covered and when the sun shone, they were a brilliant white against a rich blue sky. Streams from melting snow were catapulting downhill, and wildflowers provided splashes of bright color in the new spring grass just appearing on the mountain pastures.

A Jewish family had rented a place close to ours, and I found myself often looking toward their house. Through their windows I could see that they seemed to spend much of their time in prayer. I was particularly attracted to this scene because of their pretty teenage daughter. She seemed so vulnerable and lovely. I often thought of that girl in subsequent years and the poignant scene of her family in prayer. I wondered what fate befell them. They were facing a much greater danger than we faced.

My father's behavior during our brief mountain respite seemed quite out of character and, for some reason, I found it annoying. This man, who had seldom entered a kitchen, was suddenly spending hours just standing at the stove, stirring endless pots of milk. Perhaps this quiet activity aided his thinking processes. But to me, it appeared like a frivolous activity for someone who was largely responsible for the day-to-day decisions that affected our very survival. However, he appeared to be focused on one simple task—saving his family from the perils of drinking raw milk.

Chapter 24

To Spain (Almost)

WE DIDN'T LINGER LONG in our mountain idyll. The spring of 1940 was not the time for leisurely vacations. The news that reached us was not encouraging. Germany's defeat of France was looming ever closer. Its troops entered Paris on June 14. The Polish government had gone into exile in London. The French government, including most of the legislative branch, withdrew to Bordeaux. The commander in chief of the Allied forces, General Gamelin, was dismissed.

The story of the general's dismissal had a certain poignancy, even though he might have deserved his fate. While he and his officers—the *etat major*—were retreating toward the south, they paused to eat in a neighborhood restaurant. The restaurateur felt honored to receive such important personages and prepared an impressive repast that lasted a long time. The general was eating his dessert when a message was brought to him. He read it and abruptly got up and disappeared. His military career had just ended.

My sympathy for the man was not blinded by my lack of respect for the military strategy that he and his fellow generals and politicians pursued. Poland, the first to be invaded, had ignorance as an excuse. But it is difficult to forgive France for severely underestimating German strength. General Veygand, one of the heroes of the First World War, succeeded Gamelin and almost immediately considered laying down arms. He was pessimistic by nature and had no faith—perhaps justified—in the French Resistance.

Before we received this catastrophic news, we had already decided we must leave France as soon as possible and get to England by way of Spain. We squeezed again into our little Peugeot, said farewell to the Pyrenees, and headed for the Hendaye Road, on the border of the Atlantic Ocean near the Spanish frontier. With our destination close in view, we arrived at a bridge connecting the two countries. Customs agents from both countries were stationed at the bridge. The frontier was crowded with many vehicles that were trying to accomplish the same passage we had in mind. Cars would arrive at a desperate speed, only to end up waiting in a long line. My father, physically and mentally weary from the stress of our situation, dozed briefly during this long wait. When he woke, he seemed well rested and jumped from the car to talk with French customs officials. When he got back into the car, the customs officials motioned for us to get out of the line of cars and proceed directly toward the Spanish customs agents on the bridge. The less-favored drivers, sitting anxiously in line, must have thought we were very important and privileged people.

Once we arrived at the Spanish frontier, however, our luck abandoned us. After examining our papers, the customs agent refused to let us enter. I was driving, and with a bit of youthful cockiness, I continued to advance. Quickly, an enormous hand shot through the car window and grabbed me by the chest. With his other hand, the customs official took hold of the steering wheel and began turning it back toward the road. Faced with such unchallengeable authority, there was no choice of action. I turned the car on the bridge and retraced our brief triumphant route. The drivers who had watched us speed ahead of them must have taken great pleasure in watching our ignominious retreat.

This painful incident with the Spanish customs official was another juncture with unforeseen critical impact. If the family had succeeded in getting to England, André and I would have been ineluctably inducted into the Polish army. There were relatively few Polish refugees of combat age in England. The small number who made it to Great Britain and were able to join the combat forces were involved in some of the most perilous operations. They'd fled Poland, only for many of them to lose their lives in risky and useless operations.

A large proportion of young males of our age were either killed, or made prisoners, or sent to forced-labor camps. A Polish contingent was used to try to recapture the port of Narvik, Norway, from the Nazis—a costly operation in human life. An even more disastrous operation took place in Arnhem, Holland, where many Poles perished or were taken prisoner. That debacle left an indelible memory for all who were involved or knew of it. The plan had been conceived by Britain's Field Marshall Montgomery and approved, with reticence, by his U.S. counterpart, General Eisenhower, who wished to avoid worsening his relations with Montgomery. British and Polish airborne troops parachuted in behind enemy lines, making a heroic attempt to secure control of key bridges on the Rhine where it emptied into the North Sea. This would have opened the way for Allied troops close to the city of Arnhem. The success of the project rested on the premise that the Germans would not react rapidly. The Polish general, Stanislaw Sosabowski, in charge of the parachute detachment, asked the Allies a very pertinent question: "What about the Germans?" Indeed, what about the Germans? They had two heavy divisions situated nearby. The tragic outcome of the battle should have been evident.

Not able to enter Spain, we went back to Bayonne, the main city of the region, in order to try again to obtain visas. Before this was accomplished, major events took place that caused us to change our plans.

Between the Nazi invasion of June 14 and June 22, the uncertain world in which we found ourselves went through another major upheaval. The French prime minister, Paul Reynaud, resigned and was replaced by Pierre Laval, a former prime minister and noted Germanophile. Laval called on Marshall Petain, the great hero of World War I, to become chief of state in the National Assembly, which had relocated to Bordeaux. Petain was idolized for his role in the defense of Verdun, where the bloodiest confrontation of the First World War had occurred. But Petain, who was now serving as ambassador to Spain, was over eighty years old. The first action he took was to ask Germany for an armistice—that was June 17, 1940. Thus, the continuation of the war became impossible.

The next day, June18, was a memorable day. General de Gaulle issued a call from London, urging his countrymen to join with him in continuing the struggle: "France has lost a battle, but France has not lost the war." At this time, few French heeded his call.

On June 22, 1940, with Hitler present to savor his victory, the Franco-German armistice was signed at Fontainebleau, in the same railcar where Marshall Foch had concluded the armistice for the victorious allies at the end of the First World War. This was sweet revenge for the Germans, who wanted to erase the humiliation of the Armistice of 1918.

The armistice decreed the partition of France into two zones: the northern zone—that included Paris—where the administration was handled by the Germans, and where the occupying troops kept a tight control on all activities; and the southern, or free zone, where the quasi-independent government in Vichy had the responsibility for public order and the functioning of public institutions. Vichy, the region known for its spas and curative waters, would be known forever after for its sometimes treasonous collaboration with the Germans.

For my father, the French administration in southern France was an enormous relief. He greatly feared the German Gestapo. With its absence in the southern zone, he gave up the idea of trying to get to Spain. His older sister, my aunt Zofia Szuman, had been living in Nice on the Cote d'Azur for a number of years, and this motivated my father to think of moving there.

Chapter 25

Flight or Scenic Tour?

IT IS A LONG road between Hendaye, on the Atlantic coast, and Nice, on the Mediterranean Sea. Taking into account the heavy traffic and a certain anarchy that reigned then in France, we avoided the main route and chose the secondary roads along the Pyrenees. Not feeling very pressed, we reverted again to our tourist mode. The region was quite picturesque, sometimes even wild. We traveled east, through Basin Aquitaine, Languedoc, Lourdes, Argeles-Garzost, and Tarascon, stopping often to sightsee.

When we reached Perpignan, we knew we were close to the Mediterranean. We proceeded quickly to Cannet Beach for our first view of this fabled sea. It was a great event for us. The sea of which we had read and heard so much—the sea that was celebrated by painters and poets—was a deep indigo blue. We stood for a long time, remarking to each other on its beauty. However, I was struck by a strange spectacle. It was scarcely days since France had suffered one of the great defeats of its history, where hundreds of thousands of soldiers were made prisoners and deported to Germany, yet here, lives seemed untouched. Soldiers, appearing slovenly and often bare-chested, lounged unconcernedly at tables in the cafés and wandered leisurely in the streets or sunbathed on the beach. It was a jarring juxtaposition of callousness so short a distance from great tragedy, and one of vulgarity against a backdrop of such great beauty. On witnessing this scene, my father told me to watch over eleven-year-old Marysia, who wanted to bathe in the sea.

Once having at least dipped our toes in the Mediterranean, we continued our journey eastward, traveling through Narbonne, Montpelier, Nimes, and Arles. When we reached the university town of Aix en Provence, we made an important stop. Aix and the Academy of Aix control all the schools of the entire region, including those of the Cote d'Azur, which encompasses Nice. Ever mindful of our need to pursue our education, no matter how uncertain we were of where we would end up in a world of shifting alliances, we paused in Aix for my father to enroll André and me in the first part of the baccalaureate. It was just in time, for all French students must cross this hurdle in order to proceed to the next level of education. The baccalaureate was scheduled to take place in several weeks in all the French schools in the free zone. If we had failed to enroll at that time, André and I would have lost a year.

Once we accomplished these complex formalities, we continued our journey, stopping at the large naval base of Toulon. After the armistice, the French fleet chose Toulon as its home base, hoping it would be safe in the free zone. From a hillside vantage point, we looked down on eighty battleships weighing hundreds of thousands of tons. They towered over the surrounding landscape. The sunlight reflecting off of their metal surfaces caused thousands of points of light to sparkle in constant motion upon the water. I remember uttering a slight gasp at the first sight. It was not only their dazzling beauty but the power they represented that struck me with an almost physical impact. How unbearable it would have been if we had known, at that moment, that two years hence, the French would scuttle almost their entire fleet in order to avoid capture by the Germans.

For the last lap of our voyage, from Toulon to Cannes, we took a winding route, passing breathtaking views of the mountains and the Mediterranean coast. Our journey took us by Hyeres, le Lavandou, St. Maxime up to St. Raphael, and then along the Massif des Maures. The Massif des Maures was a low, wild mountain chain, covered with forests of pines, oaks, and chestnuts. Its steep plunge seaward took it almost to the shoreline. Further on were the Corniches des Maures, where numerous coves dotted the land's edge; then the Massif de l'Esterel to Napoule, which offered one of the most beautiful scenes in France. Rocks the color of red ochre rose in steep relief beside tiny bays and rocky inlets.

When at last we reached the Bay of Cannes, with its broad panorama of the Mediterranean, we drove along the Croisette, a famous avenue at the border of the sea with a series of grand hotels: Martinez, Miramar, Carlton, Grand Hotel, and many others. For my parents, this evoked memories of a time, still recent, when they had stayed in those hotels. For André, Marysia, and me, our thoughts were immediately of water sports and wonderful vacations at the beach.

In recalling the names of all the memorable places we passed through on our way to Cannes, I make no mention of St. Tropez. At that time, St. Tropez was a simple fishing village. Now, the whole world knows of it because the French actress Brigitte Bardot bought a villa there and launched it to fame. She was only five years old when we passed that way for the first time. Twenty years later, she became a celebrated actress with her film *And God Created Woman*, and St. Tropez suddenly became fashionable.

Our parents wanted to linger in a place that had many wonderful associations for them. Rather than the lavish hotels they were used to, we stayed for several weeks in a pleasant little hotel in Cannes. We were quite happily situated, not far from the beach. Again we were able to forget, for a while, our uncertain footing as homeless drifters in an unstable world.

This was an agreeable period for André and me, although interrupted by the first part of the baccalaureate. We took the written exams in Cannes. My good grades in math and physics compensated for my lack of language skills, especially in French spelling. Two weeks later, in Nice, we took the oral exams. I passed both exams without difficulty, but André was required to repeat the written exams. André hadn't held many illusions about his chances of passing the baccalaureate, but for our father, André's failure was a great disappointment. From our early childhood, he was determined that André and I should be raised like twins, even though André was eleven months younger and of different interests and aptitude. This meant that either André would be one year ahead in his studies, or I would be one year behind. Unfortunately for me, the latter was the case. This would have been of no importance if we had remained in Poland, but in France, it was a serious handicap to be a year behind. For the moment, however, André's failure put an end to our studying at the same level. He had to repeat a grade, and I entered the next level of mathematics in order to prepare for the second part of the baccalaureate.

Chapter 26

Temporary Shelter

IT WAS AT THIS time that our aunt Zofia Szuman, our father's older sister, reentered our lives. She was the mother of the young cousin who André and I had spent time with shortly before he died of tuberculosis at age nine. Tragically, another son's life was also cut short by the same disease when he was just twenty-one years of age. Although he was a number of years older than I was, he had been a riding companion of mine, and I remembered him quite fondly. Our aunt was never the same after the loss of two of her sons. To add to her suffering, her husband turned out to be another of those wealthy wastrels who popped up too often on our family tree. Born into a landed family of considerable wealth, he had managed to squander the entire family fortune. Fortunately, our aunt had her own inheritance, and she left her feckless husband and moved to France before the war broke out. She bought a villa at Nice in the Cimiez quarter on the Avenue de Picardie and had the family coat of arms, Tarnawa, sculpted on the villa's wall. She was living there with her two daughters when we, her itinerant relatives, arrived on the scene.

She found us an apartment on the first floor of a villa named Sandra that was situated on the other side of the street from where she lived. It was a comfortable apartment, with a beautiful view of the sea. The hill of Cimiez, overlooking Nice, was recognized for its exceptional surroundings and Gallo-Roman sites that dated back to antiquity.

Arenas from that era can still be visited today, and Cimiez has preserved its reputation as the aristocratic quarter of Nice. An abundance of beautiful villas remain, as well as luxurious apartments that were once part of grand homes. In the nineteenth century, Queen Victoria stayed there every winter in a sumptuous residence, which later became the Hotel Regina. From the time of our arrival at Cimiez, I promised myself that I would return someday to live there. It would take many years and many twists and turns in my life before that would happen.

Our move to the apartment in Nice began to have a feeling of permanence. My parents had truly had enough of their gypsy existence. After our mother's difficult and overwhelming initiation into the world of domesticity in our first months in Paris, she gradually began to adjust to her drastically altered circumstances. Now, she did the cooking and the cleaning and all the other work that used to be done for her. By the time we settled in our apartment in Nice, she had begun to accept her situation with efficiency and good humor. Our father continued to make all the important decisions, but the adjustment was more difficult for him. His anxiety over our financial circumstances and a loss of self-esteem would plague him for the rest of his life. For us children, it was still vacation time, and every day was spent at the sea—a sea that was wonderfully warm in comparison with the cold Baltic that we had been used to in Poland.

Soon, however, it was time to think of enrolling in school again—André in the eleventh grade, and me in a higher grade for students who excelled in math. This class prepared students for the second part of the baccalaureate, which would open the door to higher education. My school, which was in Nice, had an excellent reputation. It was located a short distance from Cimiez. Unfortunately, the school was not able—or did not wish—to accept André. Consequently, he had to enroll at the Park Imperial School, far from Cimiez and reachable only by long trips on a tramway. Our father found it unacceptable that we were not attending the same school, even though our classes and hours were different. With enormous regret, I felt compelled to submit to my father's wishes and change to André's school.

Our father's treatment of André and me was so rooted in the family and culture from which he came that he was quite ignorant of the damage he might cause to both of his sons by requiring them to do everything in tandem. He thought he was doing the right thing. I was handicapped by being held back, as was André, by having to pursue the same course of study as mine. André was practically forced to enter an engineering school when he would have been happier studying literature and philosophy. After having to repeat a class and not being able to advance to a higher level of mathematics, he finally was able to study philosophy, which he liked, and he passed the corresponding baccalaureate. I, on the contrary, would have been seriously handicapped if I had been obligated to follow André's interests. As it was, I later suffered the consequences of not advancing with my own age group.

We passed the first anniversary of the German invasion of Poland while living in Nice. Until that anniversary, we had been able to get along quite well in comparison to many others. We were alive and living in beautiful surroundings, and André, Marysia, and I were able to attend school. The crucial decisions were made day by day; nothing was planned in advance. Somehow, we all landed on our feet. The French adage that *le hazard fait bien les choses*, ("chance makes things right") certainly described our situation.

Between September 1, 1939, and September 1, 1940, the world changed dramatically. The war had already been lost in continental Europe. Poland, France, Belgium, Holland, Luxemburg, Denmark, and Norway were all at the mercy of their invader. Nazi forces, and sometimes Italian Fascists, had occupied the conquered countries. The people in those countries, who had survived death or capture had their lives turned upside down.

Everything depended upon Great Britain, the last bastion of resistance against the Nazis. But how long could it hold out? As soon as Hitler had France under his control, he concentrated his attention on England. Marshal Goering convinced Hitler that massive bombing would break the morale of the population and destroy British industry. It was hoped that the air raids would eliminate the advantage held by the superior British navy and make a risky invasion by sea—Operation Sea Lion—possible.

Beginning in August 1940, England was subjected to daily bombings, focused at that time on the large cities, particularly London, and the main industrial centers, such as Coventry. The results were alarmingly effective. Part of London was in flames, and industrial production was seriously hampered. From France, it appeared that the end of the English resistance was near. French citizens who had collaborated with the Germans were convinced that they had bet on the right horse. Their future careers seemed assured. My father, who knew the English better than he knew the French, remained confident. I remember his saying to us, "The English will never give up." He was right. By the end of 1940, the bombing of Great Britain had stopped. The British Royal Air Force was actually winning the air war. The Luftwaffe was suffering excessive losses. The contemplated sea offensive against England never took place. Hitler shifted his emphasis to other theatres. He began a massive buildup for a grand offensive against the Soviet Union.

Poland, meanwhile, continued to suffer more deaths, more missing persons, and more deportations than in other countries, for it was suffering not only from the Nazi occupation but from Soviet atrocities. Our repeated attempts to make contact with Zygmunt and Stephanie failed. Fear and anxiety over their fate was ever present to temper whatever relief we felt over our own circumstances, as tenuous as they were.

While we felt reasonably secure in Nice, our parents felt compelled to take account of our situation. Our wealth in France consisted mainly of the jewels we had carried, hidden on our persons, as we traveled. We had no idea how long the war might last, nor whether we would ever be able to recover any of the wealth we left behind in Poland. It was necessary to sell jewels in order to live and sustain our family. This led to a disastrous misadventure.

The persecution of Jews, which had begun in Germany, was extended to every country the Nazis occupied. In France, Petain's Vichy government assisted in their persecution. Cimiez had been home to many well-off Jews before the war. Now, they had no thought but to flee the Nazi terror. Departing Jews left most of their wealth behind them. I remember commenting to my father that one could buy veritable palaces in Cimiez at pathetically low prices. But we had no idea which way the winds of war would toss our little family. My father had neither the interest nor the resources to shop for palaces at bargain-basement prices; he was searching for buyers for our cache of jewels.

His search eventually turned up reliable information on a Jewish man, fleeing Nazi persecution, who wanted to leave France carrying jewels, which were easier to hide than other forms of wealth. A rendezvous with this man was arranged to take place in Marseille. My father had such a fear of being taken for a Polish Jew that he always tried to avoid any unnecessary exposure, so he hired someone to carry out the mission for him. His emissary was André Rigoine de Fougerolles, a former French cavalry officer, who was engaged to marry Aunt Zofia Szuman's daughter, Zonia.

The transaction was expected to yield around one million francs. Not surprisingly, André de Fougerolles didn't want to have that much money on him any longer than necessary, so when he reached Marseilles, where he had to spend the night, he postponed the transaction until the next day. When he arrived at the appointed rendezvous the following morning, his prospective buyer had disappeared. A roundup of Jews had occurred during the night, and the buyer was either arrested or had gone into hiding. The whole affair had fallen apart. André de Fougerolles returned from Marseilles empty-handed. My father was devastated. It took him a long time to get over this experience. An opportunity like that never came again. The jewelry was sold off, bit by bit, at far below its value.

While our father struggled to come to terms with this disappointment and figure out what to do next, we each had to deal with our own pressures and circumstances. No matter what was happening, it was necessary for me and my siblings to continue with our schooling. In the autumn of 1940, I enrolled in the high school in Nice. All the subjects were challenging and interesting. Even better, we had an excellent teacher—exacting and severe but appreciated by the whole class. Sadly, this professor was Jewish, and for the Germans and their lackeys, the Vichy government, it was intolerable that the Jews occupy teaching positions. He had to leave in the middle of the school year, and someone quite hopeless replaced him. I resolved not to let this set me back and began working on my own. I studied all the chapters necessary for the baccalaureate, as well as those at an even higher level. I sought help in this effort by contacting the departed professor and taking private lessons at his home.

On taking leave of him at the end of the last lesson, he said, "You are, of course, going to prepare for the *Concours aux Grandes Ecoles.*"

"Alas, no," I replied. "I am too old." Late in the school year, I had learned of an age limit of which I had been ignorant until then. I had thought I had a good chance of entering the Polytechnique, but I would have had to pass the "bac" at age seventeen years—preferably sixteen—in order to advance to the Concours for the Polytechnique. Because my father had held me back to be on the same level as André, I was a year and a half too old. I had come up against the rigid French educational system.

In the spring of 1941, I passed the baccalaureate exams and began looking for an engineering school. Neither my father nor I had any idea how to go about it. Again, just by chance, I found what I was looking for. The Ecole Centrale Lyonnaise offered a four-year program that was open to high school graduates like me. The first year was a preparatory year, and the final year was devoted to specialization in either electrical or mechanical engineering. Lyon was the largest city in the free zone, so my father accepted my proposition to continue my schooling there.

Even though André still had to finish his last class of philosophy in high school, my father was determined that we should remain inseparable. Several months later, in the autumn of 1941, André and I left for Lyon. Had we known what lay ahead, our steps might have faltered.

Chapter 27

Hunger, Cold, and Sickness

LYON IS AN ANCIENT city dotted with archeological sites and vestiges of its Roman conquerors. It is also the seat of important industries. It once had a flourishing silk trade, manufacturing and exporting silk all over the world. It is the second largest city in France, situated at the country's center of gravity where the Rhone and Sonne rivers join. From there, the Rhone continues its journey to the Mediterranean.

Before the war, Lyon was considered a rich city. The silk trade was still thriving. The cuisine of Lyon was famous. The well-known restaurants, such as Mère Brasier and Mère Fillou, rivaled the best Parisian tables. However, discretion being the first quality of the people of Lyon, they kept any evidence of wealth and an opulent lifestyle well hidden. Thus, in the chic quarter of La Tete d'Or, the buildings were slightly decrepit, and entry halls appeared modest. But when one entered the interior, one discovered exquisitely furnished apartments.

For my part, I experienced nothing of the opulence of Lyon. Indeed, there was little opulence left for anyone in Lyon. My four years there can be summed up in three words: hunger, cold, and sickness. It was said at the time, "The Germans are starving France." This was literally true. Everything was confiscated to feed the war machine of the Reich. Lyon was one of the areas that suffered particularly acute shortages.

The students who lived with their families fared better because of their families' access to the black market. But those of us who had to find nourishment in the cafeterias and other cheap restaurants were, in effect, dying of hunger. Our parents were, of course, sending us packages, but this was a mere trickle in a vast, dry pond. They couldn't do more, for Nice was also suffering acute shortages. The Germans not only starved the French, they also pillaged every means of heat. As if by magic, the coal, the petrol, the wood, and the gas suddenly disappeared. Lyon was very cold in the winter. The houses were not heated, and the classrooms and amphitheatres were inadequately heated. The situation was not conducive for study. The science faculty's library was the most comfortable room, and students would gather there, huddled close together, to share body heat.

André and I had to take lodgings wherever we could find them, and we were often separated. I changed lodgings frequently, each time hoping to improve my situation but generally finding myself in similar or worse circumstances. When at home, I often worked in bed, fully dressed and covered with everything available.

The worst experience was a room on the seventh floor with no elevator. I rented it from a mother with young children, whose husband was a prisoner of war. In order to augment her meager finances, she rented me her room and slept in the bathroom on a folding bed that she installed each evening. As this was the only bathroom, it was inconvenient to say the least. Often, a pitcher and bowl were my only water source. Sometimes the water in the pitcher and bowl froze, and I couldn't wash or shave. For whatever comfort it offered, my classmates were not any better off than I was.

In spite of suffering from hunger and cold, I was determined to let nothing stop me from excelling in school. The universities in Lyon had important resources in all areas of study: science, literature, law, medicine, and specialized technical schools. So I did something that few students did—upon entering the Ecole Centrale Lyonnaise, I enrolled also at the science faculty, in order to prepare for the license certificates of the upper-level studies.

There was, however, one problem—my class hours often overlapped. Although all the schools were located in the same area, it was impossible to be in two places at the same time. I made the best of the situation by working sometimes from the textbooks, without attending class. This wasn't possible, however, for the lab classes. Thus, it took me two years to pursue the general physics certificate.

The author of the two volumes on which I especially relied had been a professor at the University of Lyon, although he was no longer there when I enrolled. He had been dismissed because he was Jewish. His replacement did not attach much importance to the standard studies but devoted the majority of his teaching to the area where he felt he had made important scientific contributions. Almost instinctively, I ignored his course and devoted myself to the basic books of the dismissed professor. When the oral and written exams were given for the general physics certificate, they focused on the standard studies contained in those books that I chose to study. For the majority of the students, who had followed the replacement professor's course of study, the results of the exam were a disaster. But I passed with ease.

When I look back upon my years in Lyon, I marvel that I was able to persevere and succeed. Several weeks after settling there, I began to develop painful red patches on all my extremities: hands, feet, toes, even my nose. My hands were swollen, and my skin was so dry that cracks formed. The doctor shook his head. "Chilblains due to cold and a lack of fat in the diet."

"Will it kill me?" I asked.

"Probably not," he replied. "It shouldn't last." But alas, the patches made my life miserable for a long time. Malnutrition also caused a host of other problems, among them a throat inflammation from which I couldn't recover. Then, there were periods when I was extremely weak.

One time on the train from Lyon to Nice, I felt so faint that I had trouble standing. Fortunately, André, who didn't pursue his studies to the point of collapse, was holding up better than I was and was able to help me get off the train. My mother, on seeing me in this state, let out a horrified cry and rushed to hold me. "It's all right." I assured her. "The doctor says I will live."

I think what helped me to survive were the vacations our family spent in the villages situated high in the Southern Alps. The air was good, and the food was relatively abundant (with the help of the black market). But just like prisoners of war after being liberated, I had a problem digesting the richer food. The digestive system adjusts to starvation, sometimes with the atrophy of certain organs, and it is difficult to establish a normal regimen of alimentation.

In spite of my digestive problems, I was able to benefit from the restorative powers of the more healthful living conditions and the comforting presence of my family during these vacations. The few bright spots in my memories of the bleak and difficult war years are of those times spent in the beautiful Southern Alps.

We made excursions to St. Martin d'Entrannes and the Col de la Cayolle where, at an altitude of 2,300 meters, we had an unobstructed view of the chain of the Alps of Haute Provence and the Lac d'Alles. My father tried to swim there, but at 2,300 meters the water was too cold. We also spent time in Bueil, accessible only by following the spectacular Gorges de Cians, which resembles a miniature Grand Canyon. On another trip, we went to St. Etienne, a magical place of turquoise-blue mountain lakes that reflect the surrounding snow-covered peaks. Then, at St. Martin Vesubie, at more than three thousand meters high, we could see la Cime du Gelas on the Italian border. We hiked close to the summit, but the lack of necessary equipment—and my mother's reluctance to continue—prevented us from reaching our goal. When I think back on this, I marvel at the recuperative powers of the young. I arrived at the Alps, barely able to stand, and after a short rest with fairly adequate food, I was able to hike and climb without any difficulty.

Aided by my improved health, I also managed to continue to focus intensively on my schoolwork, even while vacationing. I felt I needed to take advantage of a temporary surge in energy before sinking again into a life of extreme deprivation. Each time I left the Alps, I wondered if I would have the strength to make it through another long stretch of hunger and cold.

Chapter 28

The Gestapo in Our Midst

W HEN I RETURNED TO Lyon, I returned not only to a life of physical deprivation and hardship but to the perils of living in an occupied country and the ever-present fear of whatever new terrors the war would bring. Although Lyon was situated in the so-called "free zone," the Gestapo were an ominous presence, ever in our midst. They were both discreet and effective. One never knew who might be arrested—or who might simply disappear.

From June 18, 1940, when General de Gaulle broadcast an appeal to his countrymen, the French Resistance began to play a growing role. It took many forms: sabotage of communication lines; attacks on German units; information on troop movements; the building of defense lines; and, as much as possible, the demoralization of the enemy. At a certain time, Lyon was at the center of the Resistance. The leader was Jean Moulin, a former government administrator.

The story of Jean Moulin's heroism is well known in France. One of a wide network of his compatriots was arrested and tortured and used by the Gestapo as bait, in order to capture Moulin. This hapless individual was forced to sit in a visible place on a busy commercial street, ostensibly reading a newspaper, with a member of the Gestapo seated beside him. When members of the Resistance passed by, he engaged them in conversation. In one such encounter, the date and place for a meeting was revealed. Jean Moulin was presiding over that meeting when the Gestapo burst into the room and went on a rampage, breaking up the furniture and beating the participants. This was but a prelude for what was to follow—torture, and then death as the final outcome. For several weeks, Jean Moulin suffered the most extreme torture, but to his last breath, he never gave in, refusing to reveal any names or information to the Gestapo. He is so revered that a university and many schools, streets, and squares have been named after him.

As for what happened to the man whom the Gestapo used as bait, members of the Resistance wanted revenge and prepared a jar of jam for him that contained poison, but their gift couldn't be delivered. After the war, he was condemned for his collaboration with the Gestapo, but the tribunal judge released him, saying that the torture he suffered constituted extenuating circumstances.

Two years after our arrival in Lyon, I moved into a little family pension. The student in the neighboring room was a Polish friend whose father was well acquainted with my parents. He was an intelligent boy, likeable, and quite athletic. A little time after his arrival, he became interested in the activities of the Resistance and began helping at clandestine meetings. One day, he didn't return to the pension. When days went by without his return, I thought that he was participating in a secret mission. But some time afterward, his father arrived, quite upset and searching for him. When I told him of his son's involvement in the Resistance, he was stricken. He spent months waiting for his son's return. but that was never to be. His son died in a Nazi concentration camp, ravaged by hunger, cold, and illness. His father, who had placed so much hope on his only son, never recovered from this tragedy.

Such tragedies played out by the thousands every day. The enormity of it was too much to face. But when a personal connection brought it up close, the fragile emotional shield that kept us from living in despair was pierced.

We were to learn later of another tragic drama that took place at the same time as the disappearance of my friend in Lyon. Our family had become acquainted with the great Polish portrait painter Boleslaw Barbacki when he did my father's portrait. After the Nazi occupation of Poland, Barbacki had some sporadic contacts with members of the Polish Resistance. He was spotted by the Gestapo and was arrested, tortured, and released, only to be rearrested when a suitable pretext was found—the assassination of a German soldier served the purpose.

Barbacki was among twenty distinguished Poles who were arrested and executed. At sunrise, in open country, one chained to the other, they were lined up along a trench that Jews had been forced to dig during the night. A worker at a nearby factory observed the scene as he hid behind a large chimney. He said the entire time the firing squad was shooting, its victims sang the Polish national anthem. The sound of their singing didn't vanish until the execution was completed.

A group of German artists had addressed a petition to the local head of the Gestapo, imploring them to spare the painter. The authorities hid the petition and pretended it came too late. Barbacki was one of innumerable Poles of great talent and promise who was exterminated, not on the field of battle but at the hands of the Gestapo. With their deaths, an irreplaceable part of Poland's patrimony was wiped out.

Miraculously, the life-sized portrait of my father survived the war. It was found in the Warsaw ruins after the war and hangs today in my office. Like most of Barbacki's works, it is a masterpiece. It is such a good likeness and so natural that my father appears ready to step out of the portrait. He is looking straight at the viewer with a hint of a smile on his lips and the resolute look in his eyes of someone who is confident of his command of events. That was a confidence that would erode with the eventual dramatic change in our circumstances.

Another Polish painter of world renown, Boleslaw Czedekowski, did a portrait of my mother in the spring of 1939, several months before the outbreak of the war. That portrait also remains in the family's possession. Czedekowski had a successful career painting the portraits of world-famous subjects, including Charles I of the Hapsburg dynasty, the last ruler of the Austro-Hungarian Empire, and General George Patton, who led the U.S. Third Army across France into Germany after D-Day. Czedekowski was more fortunate than Barbacki—he got out of Poland just in time.

Like Czedekowski, some of my parents' Jewish friends had wisely anticipated the coming Holocaust and managed to emigrate before it was too late. The largest Jewish population in Europe was in Poland. They made up about one-third of the population of many cities and sometimes 50 to 70 percent of smaller towns. Nazi death camps were set up to systematically wipe out the entire Jewish population. One of the great horrors of the war was the methodical extermination of

Polish Jews. I was later to learn that the Jewish history professor who had taught André and me was one of the victims of such atrocities. He lived in the Warsaw ghetto with his wife and eight children. They were all killed.

Chapter 29

Turning Points

ALTHOUGH WE LEARNED OF many of the atrocities in Poland only well after the fact, daily radio broadcasts from London kept us abreast of the major events in the war. In June 1941, several months before André and I moved to Lyon, we learned of the launching of the grand Nazi offensive against the Soviet Union. Hitler apparently expected a swift victory, as in Poland and France, although he surely must have known what had happened to previous invaders who lingered too long in Russia. He did occupy immense territory and take millions of prisoners, but the Russian winter arrived before he could achieve his goal. The German soldiers were bogged down in snow and mud and not able to reach Moscow.

In the spring of 1942, the offensive began again, and the Wehrmacht made further heavy advances into Soviet territory. Resistance grew on several fronts, and German progress was seriously halted. The decisive encounter took place at Stalingrad on the Volga River. Hitler was determined to occupy Stalingrad. Ferocious battles continued into mid-winter. There were enormous losses on both sides. The clashes between the two titans, Nazi Germany and Stalinist Russia, had no precedent in the history of humanity—not in the hundreds of thousands of combatants involved, nor the means employed: thousands of tanks, hundreds of war planes, and immense battlefields. The Soviet Union suffered more loss of life than any other nation. They lost twenty-five million people in the war they call the "Great Patriotic War."

By the beginning of 1943, the Soviets had encircled the German Sixth Army, which had been charged with the capture and destruction of Stalingrad. Hitler's refusal to give up would cost the lives of 400,000 men, the loss of considerable materiel, and compromise the success of the war against the Soviets. In fact, Stalingrad marks the turning point on the Eastern Front. The initiative was now in the hands of the Soviets. I remember the moment, as I listened to the radio in Lyon, when I heard of the Nazi defeat at Stalingrad. It was at that point that, for the first time, I became confident of the final victory of the Allies.

Meanwhile, the end of 1942 was marked by other major military operations. In November, the Allies had landed in Morocco and Algeria. It was the first step of an offensive that, in less than two years, would lead them onto French soil. When the Allies landed in Africa, the Germans reacted very quickly by invading the French free zone. The Allies tried to achieve the departure of the French fleet from Toulon, but on November 27, on the orders of Admiral Darlan, the fleet was scuttled in order to avoid German capture. Only three years before, we had gazed down from a vantage point above the sunlit harbor at Toulon and had been dazzled by the sight of that great fleet at rest. I was stricken when I heard the news. Seventy-three ships, including cruisers, destroyers, torpedo boats, submarines, and one battleship, were lost. In Algeria, Admiral Darlan had just engaged French Africa on the side of the Allies, but he was regarded as a traitor by some. He was assassinated by a Gaullist and was replaced by General Giraud. At Vichy, the Germans had taken hold of all levels of command. Marshall Petain and his prime minister, Laval, had largely lost their autonomy. With the occupation of the free zone, the German army spread throughout central and southern France. Thus, from the end of 1942, we saw numerous German soldiers in the streets of Lyon.

The presence of German soldiers failed to inspire me with feelings of hatred, in spite of all the atrocities that the Nazis had committed in Poland. These soldiers, like so many soldiers throughout history, were just ordinary people who were caught up in the sweep of events that were largely out of their control. Some had undoubtedly volunteered but many were conscripted. From my perspective as a young student, the German soldiers were especially notable for their amorous exploits. At that time, André and I were renting a room in a private home from an old Lyonnaise family who, like many families, had been impoverished by the occupation. At the side of the house was a windowless storage room, where the owner had installed a kind of folding bed for a young girl hired as a maid. Sunday was her day to go out, and one Sunday evening she failed to return. The owner, who was quite mean, even to her renters, was furious. Monday was laundry day—an especially heavy workday. The young maid, looking quite happy, didn't return until the following Thursday. Our apartment resonated with the owner's reprimands: "And to do that with a *boche!* You are going to see what will happen to you now!" The girl's only justification was to say, "He was so nice." As the girl didn't speak a word of German, I deduced that nature could trump any culture gap.

While the regular soldiers didn't inspire fear and hatred, the German police, the Gestapo, were a very different matter. They were the ones who caused fear and hatred. We always tried to avoid their sinister presence on the streets of Lyon. They walked in threesomes in order to be secure from assault by members of the Resistance. They wore a distinctive inscription on their chests, engraved on a metallic plaque that made it visible from afar.

After the liberation in 1944, a neighbor, who was a good hunter, boasted of having killed three members of the Gestapo. He put the plaques they had worn around the collars of three large hunting dogs and proudly paraded them in the streets of Lyon.

The occupation of the free zone by the army of the German Reich coincided with the beginning of the decline of Axis forces—German, Italian, and Japanese. This decline continued throughout 1943. Although the German armies occupied almost the total of Europe, the Allied forces continued to stop the German divisions on all war fronts.

On the eastern front, after the German defeat at Stalingrad, the Red Army began the reconquest of immense territories that were occupied by the Wehrmacht. On the western front, the Allies had landed in Italy and progressed toward the north of the peninsula. Italy's Fascist dictator, Benito Mussolini, had to resign, and his replacement, Marshall Badoglio, declared war on Germany. Roosevelt, Churchill, and Stalin held a conference in Tehran to coordinate the war and to begin to prepare for the peace. On Roosevelt's return, he declared in a speech to the American people, in words that carried heavy import, "I don't wish to speculate on the end of the war, but I can assure you that the routes leading to Berlin, Rome, and Tokyo have been considerably shortened." When we heard this speech on a broadcast from London, it gave us heart to persevere. We felt strengthened by the belief that one day, not too far away, we would again have enough food and fuel to eat and keep warm.

Meanwhile, however, the Allied successes, first in Africa, then in Italy (where the war was raging), had the unfortunate consequence of contributing to our misery. This was the time when the Allied bombings began—the Americans by day, and the English by night. Their objectives were, among others, the lines of communication—particularly the train stations and the train yards. Unfortunately, Lyon was one of the centers for the transport of soldiers and military equipment. The Perrache train station and the bridge on the Rhone, which were very close to the Ecole Centrale and to the University, were subjected to some of the most intense Allied bombings.

One day André returned to the apartment, white and trembling and suffering from nervous shock. He had almost been killed when American squadrons, operating in full daylight, dropped their bombs slightly off target. They fell perilously close to him, and he just missed being struck. The deafening noise and the sight of the dead and injured were terrifying. For months afterward, when he heard bombs falling, even far away, he searched desperately for shelter.

For my part, I escaped this experience, but another was waiting for me. In the Lyon region there was a very important train-switching yard that contained warehouses and repair workshops. The damage caused by the air raids to war materiel and to the means of communication drove the Germans to try to think of new ways to discourage the Allies from striking certain targets. One such method was to place French people at strategic places of heavy bombing. It was hoped that the prospect of killing large numbers of innocent French would make the Allies hesitate to drop their bombs. Thus, the Vichy government, operating under the direction of the Germans, conscripted me to work in the train yard at night. My work required that I walk the length of the tracks, traversing the shunts and passing the warehouses and workshops. Traces of bombs were very visible, and specialized workers were there to make repairs. I would often see trains passing through. One time, my attention was drawn to a train with a Red Cross sign. I soon realized that it was a hospital train, carrying the wounded. There were also refrigerator cars that carried the dead—probably from the Italian battlefields. The cars were lighted and as I glanced through the windows, I could see the German nurses tending the wounded. I quickly had to turn away. One look at the suffering and the human discards from the fields of battle convinced me that war was an abomination.

By luck or chance, my nights in the train-switching yard were calm. I passed *entre les gouttes* ("between the drops"), but I lived in fear that each night might be my last. By another bit of good fortune, the nights in mid-winter were freezing, and I fell ill, and my job was terminated.

Chapter 30

The Occupation—
Ever More Dangerous

A T THE SAME TIME that André and I were suffering under the German occupation in Lyon, our parents had to face a new situation. For some time, Nice had been under the control of the Italians, who were very friendly occupiers—maybe too friendly. My parents rubbed shoulders with them, quite amicably, in restaurants. They were a bit too amicable toward young girls, and it was necessary to keep a constant eye on our sister, who became the object of the attention of Italian soldiers and even of their officers. The climate changed rapidly with the arrival of the Nazi commandos. They were charged to put the situation in order, and their first priority was to liquidate the Jews. Roundups of Jews in Nice and elsewhere were on an alarming increase. There was enormous booty to be gained, because many elderly Jews of substantial means, who were not able to expatriate, were living still on the Cote d'Azur.

From the time of our arrival in France, my father had feared that he would be mistaken for a Polish Jew. Indeed, his fear was realized when the French police, operating under the orders of the Germans, arrived at my parents' door, asking for him. Fortunately, he was away, and my mother told them that he had left the area. When he arrived home, my parents left almost immediately. But where were they to go? The isolated holiday resort of the previous year, Bueil, seemed like a good idea. It was situated at 1,400 meters altitude and could be accessed only by a poorly maintained, sinuous route along the magnificent Gorges de Cians. There was little chance that the Germans would venture into this wild region.

My parents found lodging in a little farmhouse, quite primitive, near the small village of Bueil. The toilets were outside, and the only water available came from a well. Cooking was done on a woodstove in the kitchen. It was an even more radical change from their former lives, but living conditions seemed unimportant, when weighed against the sense of security that was gained.

In fact, they enjoyed the healthy air, the absolute calm, and the magnificent views. My mother scarcely complained about passing so much of her time peeling potatoes, which were their main form of nourishment. Photos of this period show her at this daily task. The time they spent in Bueil confirms a well-known truth—that one can be as happy in a simple farmhouse as in a palace.

The following year, my parents left their hideaway and moved to Allevard les Bains in the Grenoble region. I can't recall why they chose to make this move. There must have been some compelling reason, for it put them right back in harm's way. The only explanation is that they wanted to be closer to André and me—that they feared for our safety and were unable to keep in touch with us when in Bueil. Their move brought them close enough to Lyon that André and I were able to travel there frequently by bicycle.

Allevard is a resort at a moderate altitude, surrounded by mountains. Members of the Resistance were very active there—there were veritable nests of Maquisards. With the approach of the German defeat, the French Resistance movement became more audacious. The Germans responded in a manner that was filled with desperation and vengeance.

One time, when I was visiting my parents, the Germans showered the village with light bombs, simply as revenge against anyone who might be supportive of the Maquis. One bomb fell at the noon hour on a building that faced our dwelling. It pulverized the tile roof and caused a heavy tile to fall on the head of a young boy. This occurred right before my eyes, and today, decades later, I still can see the scene. The boy fell unconscious, with blood flowing from his head and running onto the sidewalk. His mother rushed to the scene, screaming for help. Several minutes later, a Maquis car arrived like a whirlwind and transported the unconscious boy and his mother away, presumably to a hospital. Did the boy survive? I never knew.

In this period of the war, I realized how precariously one's destiny rested in the hands of chance. One day, early in the morning, as I was looking out the window, I saw a detachment of soldiers running at full speed, chasing and catching any men they could find. If I had been in the street at that moment, my parents wouldn't have seen me again.

Chapter 31
Fifteen Days in Hell

IN THE SPRING OF 1944, the vise tightened more and more on the Grand Reich. On the Eastern Front, the Red Army, after taking Warsaw, advanced toward the west and targeted the Oder River. It was the last great obstacle before reaching German soil and the city of Berlin. In Italy, the Allied forces were approaching Rome, which would fall on June 4. The defeat of the Reich seemed more and more certain, but Hitler was determined to battle to the end.

The Germans faced an ever-mounting labor shortage. They not only needed to replace the millions of dead and wounded on the battlefield, but they also needed to maintain a labor force to feed the war machine. In all the countries occupied by the Reich, workers were conscripted into forced labor and assigned to the war enterprises. In France, the Vichy government was ordered to establish an organization for this purpose. This detested and feared organization was called STO, or *Service de Travail Obligatoire* ("Service of Obligatory Work"). As time passed, the Germans exerted ever-increasing pressure on the administration to recruit more workers. It resulted in a manhunt to satisfy the quota imposed by the Germans. This hunt took place not only in the streets but also in the houses. Thus, a misadventure—although this term is too feeble—befell me in the spring of 1944.

I was living alone at the time, for André and I couldn't always find living quarters together. One day, I was by myself in the apartment.

The landlady had left, and her children were in school. As the end of the school year was approaching, I was calculating my grade average from the oral and written exams at l'Ecole Centrale. I was anxious to determine my class standing and was feeling very pleased with myself, for I was sure that I would be second in my class. The first position escaped me because I had missed lab classes and industrial design in order to pursue simultaneous studies at both the Faculty of Sciences and l'Ecole Centrale. I had just finished my calculations when a strident ring announced someone at the door. Without thinking, I foolishly opened the door a crack. Two French police, working under the orders of the Gestapo, shoved their way into the hall, barking orders, "Your name! Your papers!" Then, "Follow us!"

"Where are you taking me?" I asked. They only replied, "You'll see. Take some of your personal effects." Fear so clouded my brain for a while that I have no memory of what transpired until I found myself in a prison cell. Then I looked about me and tried to gather my wits.

I am convinced that modern prisons are like three-star hotels in comparison to the prison in Lyon at that time. It was a sordid and abominable place. I was put in a cell with about twenty detainees. We were crowded into a small space with wooden planks for beds. They were stacked one above another, and mine, as best I can recall, was the third level. There was no running water and just a bucket for a toilet. The filth and odor were overpowering!

After some conversations, it became clear that my companions were almost exclusively thieves and malefactors but not murderers. I was, therefore, in respectable company, and I didn't have to complain about my roommates. In fact, one of the prisoners tried to entertain us each evening by performing obscene dances. As for the food, it was inedible. It bore no resemblance to hallowed French cuisine. I scarcely ate and rapidly became weak.

Anxiety over my fate also contributed to lack of appetite. The prisoners in my cell were constantly rotating. They were called out to be interrogated, and some would return, while others would disappear. Then new prisoners would arrive. It seemed to me that I had been forgotten, and I began to wonder if I would be locked up for years. I had no way of communicating with my family, and I feared for how they would react if they discovered I had vanished.

In my weakened physical condition, and with no newspapers or any contact with the outside world, I became more and more apathetic. Then, suddenly, around fifteen days after my arrest, I was summoned. I was told that I was enrolled in the STO and had been assigned to work in an aluminum factory. My papers were returned and without further ceremony, I was out the door, saying *au revoir* to prison life.

Just as I exited from the jail, a tram that could take me to my apartment was starting to leave. I started to run toward it, but my legs buckled beneath me. I fell, shaking, to the curb, and sat there, waiting for the next tram. On my arrival home, the landlady could not believe her eyes. She had thought she would never see me again. Fortunately, my family hadn't known of my absence.

Chapter 32

A Change of Fortune

MANY MEN WHO WERE enrolled in the STO were sent to Germany, and they never returned. I had the good fortune of being assigned to a French factory. It was situated thirty kilometers to the north of Grenoble and—another mysterious bit of luck—only ten kilometers from my parents' home. This allowed me to get together with my family every weekend. When I arrived at the factory, I was received by the director of the establishment. Seeing that I was very fatigued, instead of sending me to a workroom, he gave me a job in the fresh air, where I helped to carry some rail lines into the factory.

I was lodged in the workers' village and assigned to a little house. My neighbors in the village were mainly foreigners. The men worked in the factory, and the women and young girls assembled leather gloves. It seemed there was no machinery for this type of fabrication.

My fellow workers in the factory were pleasant young men. Moreover, I established friendly relations with the director's son, who had just finished his engineering studies at Grenoble and was training in the factory. Sadly, it was a short while after I left the factory that he was killed in an accident. He was inspecting the boiler room and was sprayed by the overheated vapor from a boiler with a broken pressure valve. His death was instantaneous.

On June 6, 1944, I was working at the factory when my team and

I learned of the Allied landing at Normandy. It was a momentous day! Little work was accomplished then—or for several days afterward. The entire hierarchy of the factory, from the highest to the lowest workers, was listening to the radio. We all understood that the fate of France— and of the war—was going to play out during those fateful days.

It was dangerous to be found by the Germans and their French lackeys to be listening to news from London. Information that arrived was distorted by Nazi propaganda and full of interference. The first day, the Germans triumphantly announced that the landing beaches were strewn with millions of bodies of American and English soldiers. But by evening, we learned that certain beaches were occupied and that the Allies were beginning to land heavy materiel. The following day, beachheads were established. In the weeks that followed, the Allies brought reinforcements and progressed inland. The first objective of the landing was achieved on August 1, with the breakthrough to Avranches. When we learned of that, we knew the landing had succeeded, and the liberation of all of France would come soon. Many experts had harbored doubts, and the success of the landing was not at all certain. The obstacles were formidable.

In the three years that preceded the invasion, the Nazis used hundreds of thousands of slaves—forced labor—to build what was called the Atlantic Wall. This gigantic chain of fortifications, which stretched along the Atlantic coast and the English Channel, was equipped with thousands of heavy cannons aimed toward the sea, along with thousands of nests of machine guns and miles of communication lines, the whole of which were integrated with blockhouses of reinforced concrete to provide protection against aerial bombardment and artillery fire from Allied ships. In addition, metallic structures were partially buried along the length of the shores, constituting death traps, as much for the men who were landing as for their equipment. By all previous standards, this Atlantic Wall seemed impregnable. But the Allies improvised methods for which there was no equivalent in the history of warfare. The Allied armada consisted of not less than three thousand ships to transport the troops and supplies. Equipment of all kind, nonexistent until then, had been invented. However, the victory at Normandy was not achieved without enormously heavy losses. Omaha Beach, the most deadly, was littered with the corpses of American soldiers. Today, thousands of crosses, in the surrounding meadows and in the American cemetery at Normandy, mark the burial places of those soldiers. Each year, ceremonies are held to honor their deaths.

I sometimes ask myself if the Germans wouldn't have been able to push the Allies to the sea if the Wehrmacht hadn't committed some strategic errors. Eisenhower himself was not assured of success, as the landing was a perilous and complex operation. Many experts had doubts and were not at all certain that it would succeed. The day before the landing, Eisenhower wrote a short memo, intended for Roosevelt and Churchill, in which he took full personal responsibility for its failure. Uncertainty about the weather, which was very unstable, added to numerous man-made hazards. Rain and gale-force winds and huge waves caused a delay of one day, but there was only a narrow time frame in which to act. The invasion took place the next day, on June 6. Even with remarkable innovations and enormous military might, it was necessary to follow some of the same practices that warriors from the beginning of time had used—the invasion was coordinated with the earliest phases of the moon.

Once the armada was launched, there was no turning back. They were at the mercy of the weather. Conditions had improved in twenty-four hours, but the weather was still among the worst on record for that season.

The German intelligence service knew that the Allies were planning to land in the summer of 1944, probably in June, when the days are the longest, but they didn't know the exact place of the landing. The shores of the Channel, particularly in Normandy, seemed the most probable sites. The Wehrmacht was involved in fierce combat along the length of an immense front, primarily in the east. It could have been possible to reassign part of that front to form a powerful local force in France that was capable of responding rapidly during the landing, but Hitler was very absorbed by the Eastern Front and didn't seem to have believed in the possibility of a successful Allied invasion. When he finally responded with the necessary men and materiel in December, it was five months too late.

Marshall Rommel, probably the most brilliant officer of the Wehrmacht, was known to have said that "The first twenty-four hours will be decisive." Each hour counted, and in this case, Hitler inadvertently contributed to Germany's defeat. The night before the invasion, Hitler had gone to bed well after midnight. When the attack began before sunrise Hitler was still asleep. Marshall Rundstedt, who was responsible for the German forces, wanted to immediately move troops to the site of the invasion, but it was obligatory that Hitler approve this strategic decision. No one dared to wake up the slumbering dictator. Thus, all actions were held up for several hours, and valuable time was lost. Eisenhower's note to Roosevelt and Churchill did not have to be delivered.

It took many weeks before fifty divisions were mobilized under the command of Marshall Rundstedt. They attacked the Allied front in the Ardennes and in Alsace. Hitler hoped for a rapid victory in France so he could concentrate entirely on the war against the Soviet Union. He expected to push the Americans and English back to the sea, repeating what had happened four years earlier at Dunkirk.

In the first days, the results of Rundstedt's offensive were devastating. Profiting from the surprise effect and favored by bad weather and fog, the German air force destroyed hundreds of Allied planes. The Wehrmacht pierced the front in the Ardennes and advanced rapidly to the interior of the country. For a while, it seemed as though another defeat, comparable to that of 1940, might take place. But the balance of force was different this time. Since the landing, the Allies had gathered hundreds of thousands of men and considerable war materiel in France. It would ultimately render them invincible.

The army of the legendary General Patton, with his thousands of tanks, confronted the armored divisions of the Wehrmacht, bringing them to a stop and forcing them into a slow retreat. Heroic acts, such as the defense of Bastogne by the 101st American Airborne Division during the Battle of the Bulge, played a significant role. Bastogne was a strategic center for the Wehrmacht. The German offensive slowed the entry of the allied forces into Germany by several months, but in final account, this was but a flash in the pan without consequence to the outcome of the war.

We knew that the great leaders of the Wehrmacht, who were judging the situation with competence and objectivity, had no doubt about the eventual outcome of the conflict. Rommel, who had sustained a head wound during the invasion, advocated to Hitler a political solution to the crisis. The dictator responded by asking him to leave the conference room. It is without doubt that Rundstedt himself was convinced of the futility of his offensive, but he was careful to keep his convictions to himself. The recent fate of his prestigious colleague, Marshall Rommel, no doubt dissuaded him.

On July 20, an assassination attempt against Hitler failed, and he imposed a reign of terror, of which the Wehrmacht was the first object. All those, near or far, who were implicated in the conspiracy were accused of high treason, dragged before a court-martial, and executed. Even those not implicated, who were nevertheless aware of the preparation of the conspiracy, suffered the same fate. Such was the case for Marshall Rommel.

Because of Rommel's services rendered to the Reich, Hitler dared not attack him openly. Therefore, he dreamed up a more civil procedure. One morning, two generals of the infamous and dreaded SS (German Security Police – "Sicherheitspolizei") arrived by car in front of Rommel's luxurious home. Speaking as emissaries of Hitler, they asked to see Rommel and presented him with two options: he would be charged with high treason and court-martialed, for which his family would suffer grave consequences; or he could commit suicide. If he chose the second option, the official version of his death would be that he died of combat wounds. He would have a dignified burial, suitable to his rank, and his family would benefit from all the prerogatives of his rank. Rommel could make but one choice. He asked only to be able to speak to his son, who was then an adolescent. Then he drove away in the car with the two SS generals.

They stopped the car in the forest; Rommel was given a vial of poison and left alone for several minutes. When they returned, Rommel was dead. His body was transported to a hospital, where the director published the official communiqué of his death, which had been prepared in advance.

Chapter 33

Liberation, Celebration, and Retribution

SOME MONTHS BEFORE THESE events occurred, after taking into account the rapid advance of the Allied forces, I realized that my work in the Obligatory Work Service no longer served any purpose. With the agreement of the director, I was freed, and I rejoined my family at Allevard. This turned out to be my last vacation with my parents, my sister, Marysia, and my brother, André. For almost five years, we had lived precariously in the center of a whirlwind of cataclysmic events. Now, we were being pulled in different directions, as our thoughts shifted from a narrow focus on survival to the shape our lives would take when the relative calm of a war-free world would appear.

On August 15, we learned of the Allied landing in Provence. From this moment, the American forces began to penetrate the southern coastal cities. Marseille, Toulon, and Nice were liberated. Then came the Rhone Valley and l'Isere, near Grenoble, which were liberated a little after Allevard. On August 25, Paris was liberated. At Allevard, there was widespread jubilation. It was an explosion of joy after so many years of oppression. Crowds cheered the American and French detachments as they passed through the city. The Resistance units, the Maquisard, began leaving their hideouts in the forests and mountains and were appearing openly for the first time. When a German prisoner who had been held by the Maquis was shown to the crowd, he was subjected to insults but nothing further was done. The mood was celebratory. I felt sorry for the poor chap, who had the misfortune of being on the wrong side and was now facing possible imprisonment.

The number of Maquisards in the Grenoble region was impressive. Their ranks had probably expanded since the Allied landing in the south. They were easy to distinguish from ordinary men, not only by the arms they carried but also by the length of their pants. Because one couldn't find short pants in the stores, they had converted their long pants by rolling them up their legs. Whatever the reason for this fashion statement, our father warned André and me to never wear short pants, for fear we would be taken for a Maquisard and arrested.

While the majority of the population rejoiced over our liberation, there was a small minority who didn't feel at ease. These were the women who had given their favors to the soldiers of the Reich. It was deemed necessary to punish them in one fashion or another. Women who were known to have been of such easy virtue were dragged to the middle of the plaza, where their hair was completely shaved off. The poor creatures had to submit to the jeering and insults of the passers-by—mostly women. This lasted for several hours until, finally, their tormentors wearied. My window looked out on the village plaza, and I witnessed scenes worthy of the theatre.

Soon after, a style came in that softened this difficult period for the women with shaved heads. As if by magic, the designers launched the turban style. Because a turban completely hides a woman's hair, or lack thereof, much public shame was avoided. It is certain that the American soldiers who dated women with turbans didn't attach much importance to this detail. The turban style lasted for nearly a year—just about the time necessary to grow a respectable head of hair.

It was not only these unfortunate women who suffered for their actions; the hour had sounded for punishing all the collaborators—those who associated themselves with the Germans against the French, those who were implicated in the persecution of the Jews, and anyone else identified as a traitor. Many of the political figures in the Vichy government were arrested and tried before special tribunals, which were created for punishing the acts of collaboration with the Nazis. At the last moment, before the arrival of the Allies, the Nazis sent the principal protagonists, Marshal Petain and Laval, from Vichy to the Sigmaringen Castle in Germany. The old marshal, who was approaching ninety years of age, refused to get up from his bed. He must have been forcibly removed. One year after the fall of Germany, the two men were brought back to Paris and tried before the high court. They were accused of treason and condemned to death. Laval was shot but was unable to stand before the firing squad, having taken poison several hours earlier. Petain's sentence, during which he didn't say a word, was commuted because of his age. He was kept in perpetual detention in the fort on the island of Yeu, where he died at ninety-five years of age.

Naturally, there were some excesses in the zeal to punish collaborators. Industrialists, who were ordered to manufacture goods for the German war effort, were prominent targets. Louis Renault became the most prominent of them. The Renault car company was the dominant industry in France at that time. It was named after its founder, Louis Renault, who created the first French car in 1898. Over the years, his company had developed a diversified line of products, including the Renault tanks that contributed to the victory of the Allies in World War I. But World War II was a different story. The Germans demanded that Renault factories manufacture tanks for the Wehrmacht. A refusal would have probably accomplished nothing. The Germans would have simply found someone else to be in charge. This did not figure in the calculations of Renault's accusers. It also didn't help that Renault had made Hitler's acquaintance during a trip to Berlin between the two wars and had been impressed by the dictator. Upon his return, friends and acquaintances made fun of his fondness for often introducing the phrase "Hitler told me" into his conversations. Elements of the political left that were searching for victims in the industrial world found him to be an easy target. Renault was arrested and thrown into prison, where he died mysteriously two days later. There was some evidence that he might have been assassinated. His wife tried to learn the true circumstances of her husband's death, but she was unsuccessful.

The liberation of France was a tragedy for Louis Renault. For most, however, the restored sense of freedom and security and hope for the future was a time for celebration, ranging from quiet thankfulness to unrestrained exuberance. The landing of the Allies in Normandy had a particular significance for me—and probably for most of the

Polish refugees in France. For the Polish, Soviet Communism and Nazi Fascism were comparable. Poland had been a victim of barbarism from both. If the Allied landing had failed, one can imagine what would have happened. The Red Army, with the indirect support of the Allies, would very probably have destroyed the Wehrmacht. In fact, at the end of 1944, the superiority of the Soviet forces was overwhelming, and these forces were dangerously close to Berlin. The Oder River was the last obstacle. If the Soviets had been the victors, absent the presence of the Allies, it is highly probable that France would have become part of the sphere of countries under strong influence of the Soviet Union. Would France have willingly slipped behind the Iron Curtain? I believe so, because among the thousands of students where I lived, the Communists were numerous and were hoping to achieve their ideals after the defeat of the Germans. For them, Maurice Thorez, the head of the party, was almost a national hero. Among the various organizations involved in the Resistance, the Communist units were determined to affirm their individuality. They called themselves FTP—*Franc Tireurs et Partisans* ("Irregulars and Partisans"), not to be confused with FFI— *Forces Francaises Interieures.*

While the victory of the Allies helped prevent France from falling under the Soviet zone of influence, one man, General Charles de Gaulle, almost single-handedly prevented France from falling victim to the Communist scourge and helped to establish its place as a prominent player in the new Europe. While I was still a student in Lyon, I considered Charles de Gaulle to be a providential man for France. He was the only one who could pull together the true forces of the nation. He was the only one who was able to defend the interests of the country against the Americans and the English. He will always stand out as a great statesman who played a pivotal role in French history.

Chapter 34

Devastation and Tragedy in Poland

W HILE FRANCE WAS ESCAPING the clutches of the Nazis and Communists, a very different drama was playing out in my native Poland. In 1943 the Red Army launched a colossal offensive against the Nazis. It reconquered major centers in western Russia, such as Rostow, Orel, Kharkov, and Koursk, and it crossed the strategic river of Dniepr.

In the following year, 1944, the Soviets progressed on all fronts. By summer, they had reached Poland and moved toward the Vistula River and Warsaw. The joy of seeing Poland liberated from the Nazi yoke was tempered by our distrust of Stalin and what we'd heard of Soviet atrocities in Poland. This mistrust grew when Communist propaganda showed its hostility toward the legitimate Polish government exiled in London. We dreaded that the Soviets were planning to put an obedient Communist government in place.

When the Red Army entered Polish territory, clandestine military detachments were ready to take up the struggle against the Nazi oppressors. What I didn't know at the time was that my uncle Zygmunt Broniewski, under the pseudonym of Bogucki, had taken a major part in the creation of this clandestine Polish army, called *Forces Armées*

Nationale (FAN). Promoted to colonel in FAN, Zygmunt became a key player in the movement.

From the beginning of the occupation, Stefanie also was engaged in the Polish underground movement. She was an active member of FAN and, together with her husband, she dedicated important resources to help sustain the movement. She operated first under the pseudonym of Kowalska and then of Bugucka. The Soviets didn't look with a favorable eye upon the birth of this liberation movement, which was not Communist-inspired and wouldn't obey orders from Moscow. After the Red Army reached Polish territories, it continued to progress into the interior of the country and engaged in fierce battles with the Nazi troops. As German defenses were weakening, outlaw armed bands, generally formed of deserters, began to rampage through the countryside. A band of thirty such men was terrorizing the region around Garbow. Three houses already had been plundered and burned when Stefanie, who was alone at the time, learned that Garbow was about to be attacked. She went to the terrace and began shooting with a hunting rifle in the direction of the approaching men. One was killed and another gravely wounded. They fled, apparently believing that there was an organized resistance. Stefanie's bold and impetuous action probably saved Garbow from ruin.

In July 1944, before the advance of the Soviet front, Stefanie returned to Warsaw. The high commandment of FAN was preparing for an uprising to clear the city of Germans and speed the liberation of Poland. The Red Army finally reached the shores of the Vistula and occupied Praga, which faced Warsaw across Poland's principal river. The moment seemed to have come for launching the uprising. The FAN commanders believed that the Soviets would come to their aid and join in their efforts to liberate Warsaw, thus delivering a decisive blow against the German front.

The first days of the uprising went well; important areas of Warsaw were liberated, and the Germans suffered major losses. However, after the first surprise, the Germans dispatched heavy reinforcements. Warsaw became a theatre of death, as the out-armed and outnumbered Poles faced German armored divisions and were subjected to night-and-day bombing. During the uprising, Stefanie enlisted as a nurse, and in the bloody battles that followed, she was a heroine, saving numerous wounded at the risk of her own life.

The anticipated rescue by the Red Army never occurred. On the contrary, the Red Army didn't budge and forbade the English and Americans, who wanted to send reinforcements, from using the airport on Red territory. The Allies were limited to the role of spectators to a desperate battle that resulted in the annihilation of the uprising and the almost total destruction of Warsaw.

The price of the Warsaw uprising was terrible—in human life and in physical destruction. Those who were not killed had to leave the smoking remains of the city. Warsaw was virtually wiped off the map of Europe. When all had been destroyed, the Soviet troops crossed the Vistula and entered the deserted ruins in pursuit of the Germans, who were retreating toward the west.

Before their retreat, Stefanie was seized by the Nazis and sent in a convoy that was believed to be heading for a Nazi concentration camp. She managed to escape by jumping from a moving train, after taking advantage of the momentary inattention of her guards. Miraculously, she was not killed or gravely wounded, and she fled across the fields.

After her escape, Stefanie was able to rejoin Zygmunt. He had become commander of FAN and was reorganizing the units to deal with the Soviet victories. Operating under cover, Zygmunt and Stefanie frequently changed their hiding place. They went everywhere together—on visits to the units, getting supplies, and to troop gatherings and meetings.

Little by little, the Soviet forces penetrated the country, and the German troops abandoned the terrain. The Communist government, imposed by Moscow, seized control of the nation. A Red Polish army, formed by the Soviet Union, played the role of so-called liberator and tightened the grip on the national forces of Poland. It is certain that Stalin wanted to eliminate what remained of the Polish elite and to crush the armed forces that would be able to constitute an obstacle to Communist hegemony. A new constitution was imposed and a Communist regime was implanted in Poland. Stalin had decided that Poland would be part of the Communist bloc, in the same manner as Czechoslovakia, Hungary, Bulgaria, and others.

In the spring of 1945, Zygmunt managed to escape from the Stalinist vise in Poland and travel to France for a consultation with the exiled Polish political and military authorities. His goal was to establish contact with General Anders, head of the Polish army in Great Britain.

Before leaving, he arranged for Stefanie's clandestine departure. I met my uncle upon his arrival in Paris and at that time, he was expecting that Stefanie would soon be joining him. His plans were to go horribly and tragically awry.

Stefanie made two very risky attempts to get to the West. Her first attempt was through Hungary. She traveled for several weeks to Budapest and tried, without success, to obtain transit papers for France. Her second attempt was through Czechoslovakia, where she traveled in a crowded train with a group of Romanians. She reached Prague but was driven back by the Czech authorities that were now controlled by the Communists.

Stefanie was returned to Poland and arrested at Katowice on November 7, 1945. The Communist intelligence services had apparently been on her heels for some time. She was tried and imprisoned. Zygmunt was able to get only fragmentary news of her fate. Profoundly affected by her continued imprisonment and beyond hope of her rescue, my uncle fell ill. His health continued to decline, and he died less than four years later, on June 23, 1949. On his tomb is written the inscription: "General Zygmunt Broniewski—Hero of the Polish Resistance."

Zygmunt's last years were extremely sad. He was tormented by his wife's fate, and he was not able to do much for Poland on the political front. The German surrender and the integration of Poland into the Soviet bloc had brought to naught all hopes for an independent Poland. The Western allies had tried to protect Poland against the Communist takeover, but their efforts had failed. Stalin had clearly dictated his conditions during the meetings with Roosevelt and Churchill at Yalta and later, at Potsdam. The legitimate Polish government, established in London and presided over by Mikolajezyk, had to be dissolved. The Polish prime minister, General Silorski, a man of great valor, highly regarded by the Allies—and Churchill, in particular—was killed in a plane crash. A persistent rumor circulated that the GPU—the Soviet equivalent of the Gestapo—was responsible.

It was only after the fall of Communism and the liberation of Poland that the curtain was raised on the persecution of so many Poles. It was through the research of a historian, Dr. Lucyna Kulinska, who studied the archives of that period, that we learned of Stefanie's suffering and martyrdom. Dr. Kulinska was so impressed with Stefanie's bravery that she dedicated an etude to her, titled *Nieugienta*, meaning "inflexible." This spirited young woman who had been our riding and hunting companion—our friend and confidant—was in prison for ten years. When she was released in 1956, she was profoundly marked by the years of persecution and incurably ill with tuberculosis. She died several years later and rests in the Broniewski family tomb at the Powazki cemetery in Warsaw. It was an end that could never have been foreseen for someone born into the Polish elite and educated at Madame Plater, a famous institution in Warsaw for young girls of well-to-do families.

The archives tell the story of her life under Communist rule. After she was arrested, she was locked in the Mokotow prison in a Warsaw suburb. For months, she was subjected to interminable interrogations, threats, physical abuse, and probably torture. Most men would have broken under such treatment, but she never weakened. She revealed nothing: no names and no information. In the report of her interrogations, it was stipulated that Stefanie Broniewski, alias Bogucka, member of the National Armed Forces, had refused to give any information on its organization, its meeting places, or the names of the leaders. The report spoke of her animosity against the Soviet Union, of her opposition to the Communist government in Warsaw, and of her rejection of the Communist ideology in general. Finally, the report spoke of her haughty behavior and her contemptuous attitude toward the agents who interrogated her. She declared that she was ready to die and carry all her secrets to her grave.

She paid dearly! On December 10, 1946, the military tribunal sentenced her to eight years in prison. Luckily, one of the charges—murder of two partisans of the Red Army at Garbow—hadn't been retained, due to the intervention of elected officials in the village at Garbow. They were able to convince the judge that brigands were responsible.

Following the judgment, Stefanie was transferred to the hideous prison at Ferdon, near Bydgoszez, where her ordeal continued. Interrogations and brainwashing were fiercely pursued. It is in this prison that her second trial took place; it was held in secret in her cell. She was reproached for refusing to reveal names, for her hostility to the Communist authority, for her rebellion against the subjugation of Poland to the Soviets, and for her bad influence on her fellow detainees. The second verdict, this one confidential, was for ten years in prison.

The family tried on numerous occasions to obtain her release, but the Stalinist methods of terror were rampant in Poland. Someone as inflexible as Stefanie had to be destroyed. The story of her courage and martyrdom lives on due to the research and writings of historian Dr. Kulinska.

As for Zygmunt, it was necessary to wait forty-two years for the memory of my uncle to finally be honored. That day, September 22, 1991, a moving ceremony took place at Garbow in the presence of numerous civil and military personages, in order to pay homage to the memory of the National Armed Forces and their commander in chief, Zygmunt Broniewski.

Chapter 35

Peace and Change in Sight

THE EVENTS ON THE Eastern Front directly affected the future of Poland and, at a personal level, the fate of two very close and dear relatives, my aunt and uncle. But events for them hadn't yet played out to their grim and tragic end when, with the approach of autumn1944, our family had to separate. My parents and sister returned to Nice with a peace of mind they hadn't known for five years. The city, recently liberated, was now free of the Gestapo. My brother and I had to return to Lyon. André was in the second year of the Ecole Centrale, and I was in my third and final year at the school.

The only practical means to go from Allevard to Lyon, a distance of 140 kilometers, was by bicycle. Many of the train tracks were partially destroyed; roads were often in a bad state, and as for gasoline, there was none. With our suitcases on our bike racks, we took off for Lyon. I remember that we argued the entire way, without stopping, over how fast we should go. André, who didn't share my excessive zeal to get started on the next level of schooling, would have preferred a more leisurely ride.

We found Lyon greatly changed. With the liberation, the heavy, stifling atmosphere of the recent war years had ended. At the Ecole Centrale, as at the Faculty of Sciences, some new faces appeared. The Jewish professor and others who had slipped quietly away during the Vichy regime had returned and resumed their positions. Their replacements for those years just disappeared one day. The number of students had slightly increased, because the workers at the STO, the deportees, and even certain prisoners of the Germans, had now returned. Among those students who had openly manifested their German sympathies, the liberation constituted a difficult moment; some of them feared reprisals. The mother of a colleague at school, who was living in the same family boarding house as I was, came to see me to plead the case for her son. I assured her that I would not denounce him.

By autumn of 1944, France was almost totally liberated. The Allied forces were approaching inexorably toward the frontiers of the Reich. The end of the war was in sight; its outcome was assured. However, free of worries over the destiny of my adopted country, I managed to create some new worries for myself. Although they seem childish now, at the time they were very important to me. I wanted, at all cost, to be elected president, or *zident*, of the student association at the Ecole Lyonnaise. By tradition, this was an important and prestigious position. The zident had significant influence with regard to the education and work conditions of the students. In order to be elected, one needed to be popular with one's fellow students and to have earned their esteem. I did everything I could think of to gain the necessary popularity and esteem. I organized outings, and I participated in meetings with the director, who thought well of me, but it was a waste of time. My ambition was not realized. A comrade, with whom I was friendly, said to me, "You know, Bobby"—my nickname at the school—"you will never become zident. Suppose General de Gaulle were to visit our school; he would be received by the director and would meet the zident. It is out of the question for that person to be a foreigner." Faced with this bit of reality, I realized my efforts were useless. The person chosen was the one who had held the same position earlier but had quit school at the beginning of the war in order to participate in the struggle. On his return after the liberation, it was natural that he regain his position. I later thought my ambition to be zident had been ridiculous.

While the zident episode was harmless, another tragic-comic episode of my own making came close to disaster. The professor who taught theoretical mechanics for the license certificate at the university gave a course on the same subject, but on a lower level, at the Ecole Centrale Lyonnaise. The students at the Ecole Centrale, who had failed the written exam, were able to take a remedial oral exam. One among them seemed particularly vulnerable and had a great fear of the exam. He was a very nice person, and I felt sympathetic toward him, so I foolishly offered to take the exam in his place—I assured him that he would have an outstanding grade. On the day of the exam, I presented myself under a false name. My comrade came to witness the spectacle. The professor called me to the board and gave me a problem to solve. It was an extremely simple problem of kinetics. I solved it quickly—*en trois coups de cuillère à pot*[13] and announced the result to the professor. He became furious, saying, "You have learned by heart; you have fallen on a problem where you have learned by heart." I suggested that he give me another problem, but he didn't want to hear anything. I became irritated, the young man for whom I was taking the exam turned pale with fear, and the professor was red with anger. I almost said, "I have obtained the theoretical mechanics license with honor. How dare you accuse me of learning by heart?" At the last moment, however, I caught myself and left the auditorium. My comrade received a low grade, and I escaped being expelled.

---

13   A comparable English saying might be, "In three shakes of a cow's tail."

Chapter 36

Our Lives Change Course

I N SPRING, I PREPARED for the final exams. I remember my last physics class with the Jewish professor who had been forced to hide during the Nazi occupation. This professor had predicted the probable evolution of physics. He emphasized that besides the traditional physics that analyzes reactions between atoms or molecules, a new branch would emerge that would deal with reactions between elements inside the atoms, the electrons and nucleus. He didn't use the words for nuclear reaction—fusion or fission—that are accompanied by the emission of gigantic quantities of energy, but he wasn't far off. His prediction left me indifferent at the time, but several months later, when two atomic bombs were dropped on Japan, I remembered my physics professor in Lyon.

Those bombs wiped out Hiroshima and Nagasaki on August 6 and August 9. Japan surrendered on August 14. Germany's surrender had already taken place three months earlier, on May 7 at Reims and on May 9 at Berlin. With the axis of the belligerents vanquished, World War II had ended.

The end of the hostilities in Europe coincided with the end of my studies. With the war ended and my diploma from the Ecole Centrale Lyonnaise, as well as that of Bachelor of Science, in hand, a new phase of my life had begun. I wasn't sure which direction it would take, but I was eager to get started.

Instead of choosing to reward myself with a well-earned break, I immediately set myself another goal. I realized that without a mastery of the English language, I would be handicapped. Today, practically all engineers are acquainted, to various degrees, with English, but that was not the case in the 1940s. At that time it may have even been an exception for an engineer to have a good mastery of English. I therefore put myself to work without wasting a single day.

I did, however, allow myself to pursue my new goal at the famous health resort at Vichy. This was at my father's advice, for I was still suffering some acute digestive troubles as a consequence of the dreadfully inadequate diet during the war. My father assured me, "It will be good for your liver. Your grandfather had a cure at Vichy; I had a cure at Vichy; and you need to have a cure." With two English books and a good dictionary, I left for Vichy. I don't know if the cure worked, but I know that I was able to make enough progress in English that, with the help of the dictionary, I could read an English book and understand it. It happened that one of the books I took was a bit pornographic, which probably helped hold my interest, even though learning the English names for venereal diseases was probably of little future use.

After Vichy, I spent several weeks at Vic-sur-Cere in the coastal region, where there was a sizeable congregation of Poles. One of my companions was the father of my Lyon friend who died in the Nazi concentration camp. He had finally been able to obtain some information on the circumstances of his son's death. After this sad encounter, I returned to Nice in order to spend the last days of vacation with my parents. I then left for my place of work.

I had chosen to begin my professional life at the Societe Alsthom, Belfort, factories. In making this choice, I searched for the most important and most diversified electrical and mechanical engineering company. I felt Alsthom would provide the best professional opportunities; the choice proved to be providential. Today, more than a half century later, Alsthom is still there. Over the years, it has absorbed all its competitors and merged with the main English company in the field.

I participated in the huge effort of reconstruction and modernization in France, after the destruction caused by the years of war—an effort largely financed by the United States' Marshall Plan. I received two awards for my contributions and publications, one from the French Society of Electricians for a work titled "Problemes d'Actualite Relatifs aux Redresseurs de Mercure," and the Ampere Prize[14] for an original paper on the subject of electrodynamics. This would later lead to my heading an American research organization in Geneva, Switzerland; and the reputation acquired there took me back to Alsthom as Director of Research. Those would be splendid years, where my contribution was recognized and I was named Chevalier of the *Ordre National du Mérite*, a distinction created by General de Gaulle.

Following that, in 1977 I would spend ten years at Occidental Petroleum in the United States, working as a consultant and special assistant to the well-known international financier and philanthropist Armand Hammer. It was an exciting time, participating in major projects established by Occidental in different countries, including Poland, Morocco, China, and the Soviet Union. After Hammer's death, I would retire from Occidental and work as a consultant for two large French enterprises until my retirement from professional life at age seventy-five. But I am racing ahead. Let me go back to those first days as a fledgling engineer.

It was a long train ride to Belfort. The train system was still suffering from disorganization as a result of the war. We passed by Marseille, with a change of trains at Lyon. Happily, my bicycle that I had checked at Nice was traveling with me. On arriving in the evening at Belfort, I claimed my bicycle, put the suitcase containing all my effects on its rack, and left to hunt for my lodgings.

Belfort recently had been liberated. The streets were badly lighted. It was dark, and a light rain was falling, and I only vaguely knew the directions. I didn't dare to use my bike in the dim light. I pushed it beside me for a long two kilometers, crossing many roads before arriving at rue Strasbourg, where I had a room reserved. I rang the bell of a modest home, and an old woman opened it and showed me to my room. It was very small. A round table in the middle filled all the space left by a bed, a little armoire, and a chair. Seeing that I was wet from my walk in the rain, the landlady brought me a warm drink. This was the modest beginning to my professional life.

In the course of the following months, I decided not to return to Poland. My father, by contrast, returned to Poland in 1947. My mother and sister joined him a year later. In spite of all the bad news about life

---

14   The reader will probably recognize this name. Andre-Marie Ampere was one of several great scientists who was born and worked in Lyon. Ampere is the scientific word used to describe a measurement of electrical current.

under the Communist regime, he hoped to be able to contribute to the reconstruction of his country. This was to prove a vain ambition. As a financier and industrialist, he didn't fit in. He and a partner founded a restaurant, which was one of the rare sectors where private initiative was still tolerated. Well-organized and efficient, the restaurant was a success from the beginning. It began to compete with state-run establishments. It bothered the authorities to see such a successful example of private enterprise. My father's partner was arrested and imprisoned for fiscal irregularities. My father escaped prison, but it was necessary to close the restaurant. In order to earn a living, he organized a discreet import business of certain merchandise. The most successful item was men's ties, which were made in Poland with fabric I sent from France.

When my mother and sister joined him in Poland in 1948, the family occupied one floor of a villa in a residential quarter of Warsaw that had suffered relatively less from the bombing. Thanks to the profit from the little import business, my parents and sister had a reasonably satisfying life. Moreover, with the passing of years, the regime in Poland became a little more humane. The reaction against the intelligentsia had diminished. Social relations in Poland were less stratified. A traveler from Western Europe visiting Moscow and Warsaw was able to discern an enormous difference between the two capitols. Warsaw, although not completely free, seemed more relaxed and welcoming.

During this period, André, who had graduated from the Ecole Centrale Lyonnaise a year after me, was living in our parents' home in Paris. He was hired at the laboratory that belonged to Prince Louis Victor de Broglie, eminent theoretical physicist, inventor of the mechanical wave theory, and winner of the Nobel Prize in Physics in 1929 for the discovery of the wave nature of the electron. Admiring of his patron, André did some notable work and had an article published in scientific reviews. About this time, it happened that the government in Quebec, Canada, had built a research laboratory and was offering opportunities to young French scientists. André was not happy living alone in Paris, and he submitted his résumé. He was hired immediately. He left from Le Havre in a large ship of emigrants of all nationalities. I went there to wish him farewell. This was a sad separation. I was now quite alone, with André in Canada and the rest of my family back in Poland.

Chapter 37

The Mind Calculates; the Heart Resolves

I WAS TWENTY-FIVE YEARS OLD in 1947. I was gainfully employed and alone in my adopted country. It seemed as though it was time to find a soul mate. In the beginning, I approached this pursuit of a mate with the same seriousness that I applied to my studies in physics. However, I was soon to learn that people and relationships aren't as predictable or knowable as mathematical and scientific concepts.

In the first phase of my marriage project, I thought perhaps a Polish woman would be best—that we would share the same language and similar racial, family, and cultural origins. So, I started with a list of three prospects. I have long forgotten their names, which no doubt is a good sign. One was living in Paris, the second in London, and the third in Warsaw.

I started with the young woman in Paris. I met her at a reception given by her grandmother, a countess. She was tall, distinguished, and from an aristocratic Polish family. My preliminary contacts were sympathetic and even encouraging, but I soon began to realize that a young woman who was accustomed to the salons of Paris and a family chateau in the Loire Valley would not be a suitable wife for a young engineer who lived in a small apartment in the industrial town of Belfort.

The next young woman lived with her parents in London but visited from time to time in Paris. Our families knew each other well, even having left Poland at the same time. Her father was involved in the Polish government in exile. He followed the government when it moved to Great Britain after the French defeat. The young woman was pretty and well raised but a spoiled only daughter. There, too, I could not envisage her living at Belfort. Before going farther, I decided to explore the situation with her mother. When she told me that her daughter had just become engaged to a Polish officer in London, I was greatly relieved.

I never met the third young woman. I knew her only from photos that my father had sent me. I think he was hoping to see me return to Poland and, without even consulting me, he had begun trying to find me a Polish wife. When he found what seemed to be an ideal young woman, he began sending me photos. Soon, I received a letter from this potential marriage partner and, in spite of some reticence, I began a correspondence. Some months passed without much progress. Then, mysteriously, my father ceased to promote this union. Finally, he admitted that the ideal young woman was getting fat, and he feared that his son would have an obese wife. The correspondence soon died.

My experience with the three prospects caused me to reflect on what I had learned. I realized that I had forgotten that my family was no longer wealthy, and thus, I had to start with a very modest existence. This first stage in my professional life seemed unavoidable. I needed a wife who could accept life in a provincial town and a husband who would frequently be absent on business.

It was in this state of mind that I made the acquaintance of Eveline. She was the daughter of a deceased Alsthom engineer and had an exceptional personality. She had done some brilliant studies, had a diploma of *l'Ecole Supérieure d'Electricité* along with several other degrees, and was aiming for a PhD in one of the sciences. She lived in Paris but came often to Belfort to visit her mother. She was beautiful and had a lovely figure. She was still unattached, so I began to think about marriage. But the more I thought about marrying such an accomplished woman, the more problems I saw. In my professional career, I might have to move around a lot. If my wife had a stable occupation, this would create a conflict. In addition, although two salaries would provide a more luxurious lifestyle, I had what I confess now is an old-fashioned bias toward a stay-at-home wife.

Fortunately, I didn't have to address any of these concerns head-on. Eveline left for Great Britain for job training for several months, and our relationship withered during that time. I happened to meet her again about twenty years later and learned that she had married the French Consul General for either Argentina or Brazil.

After crossing off four prospects, I was much occupied with my work, and my nascent marriage plans went somewhat dormant. I felt, however, that it should be easy to find a soul mate near where I was living. There were a plethora of young women in Belfort in need of husbands. Local families, as well as industrialists in the region, and local business people and magistrates and other distinguished people were attempting to answer this need by organizing dancing parties. I went from time to time to these parties, especially out of curiosity but also to participate in the ordinary life of the town.

I have but a vague memory of these dancing parties, for I never met anyone who interested me, with the exception of one girl named Elisabeth, who turned out to have a very serious vice. Whenever drink was offered at one of the soirees, she always drank too much. Indeed, she became drunk. So Elisabeth was quickly crossed off of my mental list of possible mates.

I was beginning to see myself as a confirmed bachelor—until one day! It was the summer of 1951. I passed by a young woman in the street, and at first sight, I noticed that she was pretty, blonde, and very slender. That was what my head told me. My heart had another message. I watched for her each time I passed the same way, and one day, I saw her getting in a tram on her way home from work. I was driving my Renault and started to follow the tram. Each time it stopped, I stopped. It was a long route—four or five kilometers punctuated with innumerable stops. Finally, the young woman got off at the intersection of the main street and rue Cardinal Mercier, where she lived.

Once I knew where she lived, I began leaving bouquets of roses at her house. After several days, knowing that she had seen me with the roses, I ventured to speak to her. I learned that her name was Colette Dormoy, she was twenty-one years old and lived with her sister and three brothers. Her mother had died recently, and her father had died when she was just a few months old. He had fought in the First World

War in some of its epic battles, notably *Les Chemins des Dames at Picardie*. Twice he had been taken prisoner and twice he escaped. He was awarded the Croix de Guerre avec Palmes and the Chevalier de la Légion d'Honneur for his heroism. He never fully recovered from serious wounds he had received in the war and died at age forty-one.

In the days that followed, we talked more, and finally, she agreed to meet me for a picnic. Thus began a courtship that lasted almost two years. As we shared stories on how we had survived the war years, we realized that we both felt somewhat alone in the world. My family had dispersed to Poland and Canada, and she had lost both of her parents in death.

As we grew closer, all my cool and logical reasons for selecting a wife went out the window. On June 27, 1952, Colette Dormoy and I were married in a civil ceremony at Belfort and afterward, at a religious ceremony at the cathedral of Thann, a beautiful Alsace city not far from Belfort. From there, we left in my 4CV Renault—a four-horsepower car—on a six-week honeymoon. We carried a tent and all necessary equipment for camping. Our first stop was on the border of the magnificent Italian Lake Locarno at Stresa. Following this, we camped in the remote and wild Italian Alps and then went on to the Cote d'Azur in Nice and Cannes, unfolding our tent near the Lavandou. Thus began a long and happy union that cemented my earlier decision to remain in France.

****

It had been thirteen years since André and I, standing in a quiet field almost a thousand miles away, heard a distant rumbling, and felt an answering echo beneath our feet. That slight tremor was a portent of a seismic upheaval that was about to sweep through a great part of the world, carrying with it the fate of tens of millions of lives.

We were the lucky ones. We survived and were intact; those thirteen years had taken me far from where I began. It felt as though I had lived two entirely separate lives—my first seventeen years, secure and comfortable in the elegant and rarefied world of the Polish aristocracy; and the next thirteen years as a war-tossed refugee, struggling to succeed in an uncertain world and exposed to the horrifyingly ugly and brutal side of human nature.

The Poland I had known was gone, and the country where I once found only an uneasy refuge now seemed inextricably linked to my fate and future. I had learned that our destinies are shaped by much more than accidents of birth and blood. The secrets of self that remain hidden within each person's soul can triumph over the most wayward twists of fate. The resources I had discovered within myself had sustained me in some of the darkest hours. Now, with the world at peace and someone I loved beside me, I was able to contemplate the future with a light heart, ready for whatever lay ahead.

Bogdan, Vic-sur-Cère, Cantal region, Auvergne, France—summer 1944

Bogdan and Marysia at the beach—Cannes in 1910

Bogdan's mother, Zofia, peeling potatoes, Beuil, France, during World War II

Zofia on balcony at refuge in Beuil, Alpes Maritimes, France—1944

Mieczyslaw and Zofia Broniewski at Allevard, Isère, France—1944

Villa Sandra, Nice—family rented second floor during World War II

Villa Tarnawa, Nice—home of Bogdan's aunt Zofia Szuman and daughters

Bogdan and Colette, married June 27, 1952—Belfort, France

Colette Dormoy, 21 years old—Belfort, 1951

*Colette's father, Emile Dormoy, in military uniform
of the Chasseurs Alpins around 1910*

Emile Dormoy in lieutenant's uniform during World War I

Emile Dormoy (first row, second from left) in World War I military hospital for the gravely wounded

Emile Dormoy wearing the medal of the Légion d'Honneur and the Croix de Guerre avec Palmes, signifying military valor

Adieu à Emile DORMOY

Notre bon camarade, notre dévoué Emile Dormoy, conseiller général du canton d'Héricourt, est mort.

Jamais plus nous ne verrons dans nos Congrès, dans nos réunions socialistes sa loyale physionomie qui inspirait immédiatement la sympathie.

Quelle perte immense pour notre Parti Socialiste de la Haute-Saône, qui avait en lui un de ses militants les plus sincères et les plus énergiques malgré sa modération apparente.

Dormoy était venu au socialisme, après la guerre; il était de cette génération qui connut toutes les horreurs de la grande tourmente et ses convictions socialistes n'en étaient que plus solides, car il avait pu se rendre compte que seule la doctrine agissante et généreuse du Parti Socialiste était capable de donner au monde épuisé, une paix féconde et durable.

Je ne retracerai pas ici ce qui fut sa vie, toute d'honneur, de loyauté, de droiture, car tous les camarades de nos sections le connaissaient bien et cette vie simple et digne fut évoquée au cours des obsèques émouvantes et grandioses dont on lira le compte rendu d'autre part.

Ce que je puis dire, c'est qu'il possédait la sympathie générale, il n'avait pas d'ennemis, tant il était serviable et accueillant dans sa franchise native et les électeurs d'Héricourt, en l'envoyant siéger au Conseil général, en 1925, lui avaient donné une marque éclatante de leur confiance.

Combien notre Fédération de la Haute-Saône fut éprouvée depuis quelques années. En 1927 c'était Léon Jacquey, maire de St.-Loup-sur-Sémouse, que la mort emportait brutalement en pleine force et en pleine activité; en 1928, c'était Jean Lagelée, le rénovateur et l'animateur du mouvement socialiste dans la Haute-Saône, c'était ensuite notre bon Alizon, conseiller d'arrondissement du canton d'Héricourt, et aujourd'hui c'est Dormoy qui, comme Jean Lagelée est victime de cette affreuse guerre, dont les horreurs se feront sentir longtemps encore dans les larmes des orphelins et des veuves, dans tous les deuils accumulés.

Notre bon Dormoy n'est plus, nous le pleurons et son souvenir restera en nous éternellement comme celui d'un homme, d'une haute conscience morale et d'un dévouement extrême, dont l'exemple devra nous guider et nous animer dans notre action.

Il n'est plus, mais il laisse derrière lui une épouse affectionnée et cinq enfants en bas âge, dont l'aîné n'a pas plus de sept ans et le plus jeune n'a que quelques mois.

Dans notre grande famille socialiste, le devoir de solidarité existe puissamment; il est commandé par la fraternité que l'on ne rencontre en réalité que chez ceux qui peinent et qui souffrent, dont ce monde des travailleurs ou l'éducation pénétrant insensiblement la fait paraître plus belle et plus douce.

Ce devoir de solidarité, la Fédération de la Haute-Saône l'exercera pour les pauvres petits orphelins que laisse notre cher Dormoy; elle ne faillira pas à sa tâche et dès maintenant elle adresse à tous ses adhérents l'appel chaleureux dont le résultat servira à adoucir quelque peu les difficultés d'existence de Mme Dormoy et de ses tout petits enfants.

Pour la Fédération de la Haute-Saône :

Charles COTIN.

(Envoyer les fonds à notre camarade Grandjean, maire d'Héricourt, qui centralisera la souscription.)

An obituary for Emile Dormoy from a newspaper called Le Socialiste de la Haute-Saône, dated March 29, 1930

Ampère prize awarded to Bogdan for an original paper on the subject of electrodynamics, given by La Société Française des Electriciens—1954

Award created by Général de Gaulle, given to Bogdan when named Chevalier
of the Ordre National du Mérite

Marysia with Lech Walesa, Warsaw, 1965

Bogdan Broniewski, age 48, Alsthom, France—1970

Bogdan in Los Angeles office, when a member of top management of one of largest U.S. corporations

Afterword

BOGDAN'S PARENTS, MIECZYSLAW AND Zofia, returned to
live in Poland in the late 1940s. They remained there, living
comfortably though simply, until Mieczyslaw's death of a heart
attack in 1966.

Zofia returned to live in France after her husband's death. With
family members close by and surrounded by the many photos and
treasures she managed to retrieve from Poland, she lived happily for
twelve more years.

André led a somewhat troubled existence. He never ceased to yearn
for the life he had known as a boy, hunting and horseback riding in the
fields and forests of Poland. After cutting short his promising career in
France, he repeated the same pattern in Canada. He abruptly left his
job as a respected research scientist and disappeared without leaving
an address. His explanation was that he needed to "seek again the blue
sky" above his head. After great effort, his family found him, through
a Polish doctor who had taken him in.

When he returned to work again, he traveled the vast region of
Quebec as a salesman for an important manufacturer of lighting
equipment. He enjoyed considerable success and began thinking of
marrying. He made several trips to Poland, hoping to find a Polish wife,
but he ultimately fell in love with and married a Canadian woman.
When the marriage failed, he returned to live and work in France,
where he remained until he retired in his late fifties.

Free at last from the shackles of civilization, he moved to the
Pyrenees, where he spent ten happy years. He had a passion for eagles
and began writing a book on the subject. When his health declined,
he had to abandon life in the mountains. As time passed, he was more

and more subject to emotional crises and spent several months in a psychiatric hospital. He was living in a retirement home at l'Escarene in southern France when he died in his sleep at age seventy-seven.

Marysia led an eventful life that spanned several countries and two continents. After the war, she returned to Poland and lived with her parents while she completed her college education. A brief marriage to an officer in the Polish military ended in divorce. She subsequently met and married the well-known director of the Warsaw theatre Arnold Szyfman. He was in his seventies, and she was near thirty. The marriage provided her a wealthy lifestyle reminiscent of her early years and exposed her to the glamour and excitement of the theatrical world.

When she was forty-two years old, she moved to the United States to further her education and became a professor in an American university. During the fifteen years she lived in the United States, she fell in love with and married a wealthy American, Ronald Gordon-Smith. When he lost his money in a real estate crash, Marysia returned to Poland. She eventually persuaded Gordon-Smith to come live with her in Warsaw. There, he played a supportive role as a devoted husband while she dedicated the rest of her life to writing. She became the author of three well-acclaimed books: a biography of Chopin, written in 1979; the story of her second husband, *In the Labyrinth of Szyfman*; and an exquisite book about the famous eighteenth century artist, *Jean Baptiste Pillement*.

After her husband's death, when she was in her seventies, Marysia married once more, to a man thirty years her junior. Predictably, this did not turn out well. She died in Warsaw at age seventy-nine.

Bogdan is the longest lived of his family. He is sure that guardian angels have watched over him through his long and sometimes perilous existence. He has had an outstanding career, reaching the pinnacle in his field and winning recognition for valuable contributions to scientific research. After three years at Alsthom in Belfort, during which time his first two children, Corinne and Sophie, were born, he went to work for an American research organization, Battelle Memorial Institute in Geneva, Switzerland. There, he directed multinational teams in advanced research. And there, his only son, Frederic, was born. The reputation he acquired at Battelle led to his returning to Alsthom in 1962 to create and direct their research center. In the course of the following years, the center was distinguished for a number of important research programs involving collaboration with important foreign partners, such as Exxon Oil. His and Colette's youngest three children, Delphine, Alice, and Isabelle, were born during those happy and productive years.

In 1977, management changed at Alsthom, and Bogdan decided to move on. Confident of his abilities and with sufficient mastery of English, he went to the United States to look for new challenges. Soon, his achievements caught the attention of the well-known international financier and philanthropist Armand Hammer. For almost ten years, Bogdan worked closely as a consultant to Hammer at Occidental Petroleum and traveled the world as his special assistant.

After Hammer's death, Bogdan retired from Occidental and worked as a consultant for two large French enterprises. At seventy-five years of age, he retired from professional life to write his memoirs. He is currently at work on the story of his professional life. He also pursues several hobbies, notably sculpture, in which he has created beautiful works out of amber collected from the Baltic Sea.

He and Colette have had a long and happy marriage. They live in Berre les Alpes near Nice, where their six children and their families, including nineteen grandchildren and two great grandchildren, are regular visitors.

****

Miraculously, the family's once-splendid mansion at No. 25 Mokotowska survived the war and was one of the few buildings left standing among the Warsaw ruins. For a time it served as the Stefan Branach International Mathematics Center. Today it is a cultural center and historical monument that welcomes visitors from around the world. The only reminder that once this luxurious mansion was home to a family and lifestyle that have vanished from Polish soil is a bronze plaque over the entrance to the building inscribed with the name of its once proud owners: Broniewski.

Appendix A

Polish Campaign

Kampania w Polsce. (wrzesień 1939 rok)

1 Stan liczebny armii niemieckiej w 1939 na stopie pokojowej 54 dywizje piechoty, 5 dywizji pancernych, 4 lekkie; razem 1 200.000 żołnierzy. Lotnictwo 1-ej linii 4.000 samol.

2 Stan liczebny armii polskiej w 1939 na stopie pokojowej 30 dywizji piechoty, 12 brygad kawalerii, 12 bat. strzelców + cieżka artyleria i ciągi. Razem - 300000 ludzie (17 tys. ofic. 30.000 podof.). Lotnictwo 36 eskadr - 400 sam. pojowych 100 sam. rozpoznawczych.

Niemiecka doktryna wojenna :- Schlieffena i Moltke'go: zniszczenie nieprzyjaciela przy pom. szybkich i wczesnych działań frontowych, skombinowanych z manewrami oskrzydlającymi. Jest ono oparte zasadom Mayer i Bernardi, z których wynika, że "wojna jest już sama przez się tak wielkim złem że użycie najgorszych środków mogących skrócić jej trwanie jest całkowicie usprawiedliwione". (Wojna totalna, nie czyniąca różnicy między siłami walczącymi a ludnością niewinną kraju).

Polska doktryna wojenna. Ruchliwość i charakter ofensywny poszczególnych jednostek (wojna bolszewicka i kampania ukraińska, nie wym. materiału wojennego)

Zasada koncentracji sił

Dla końca lipca 1939 roku stan niemieckiej armii wynosił ok. 2 milj. ludzi. Pełna koncentr. na froncie polsk

które próbuje forsować i zagr. Warszawie; w centrum
2 dyw. pancerne wspart. art. i bombowe, przypory
front, by 9 dosięgnąć brzegów Wisły.
Na poł. V dist niepokoju Kraków, gdy 2 dyw. stamts
wie wyp. 1 dyw. Polska. -
2 Okres Przerwanie frontu i posuwanie się
wielkich jednostek zmotoryzowanych ai do
Wisły. 5–9 wrzesień

5–9 wrzei

3 dyw. zmotor., które przerwały front pod
Częst. dosięgają ostatnich linii polskiego oporu. Część
kieruje się w strony Warszawy (lewym brzegiem Pilycy) a część
zaś na wschód na Kielce i Sandomierz.
Pierwsza grupa spotyka się 6 września w ok. Rawy i Piotrkowa
z 3 dyw. polsk. w tych. mob., które rozbija i 8 września
dostaje się aż do przedmieść Warszawy (dworzec zachod.)

219

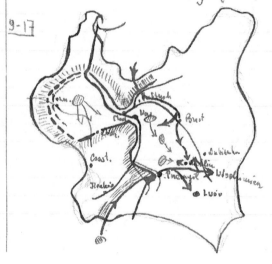

220

Appendix B
Guide Bleu Maps, 1939

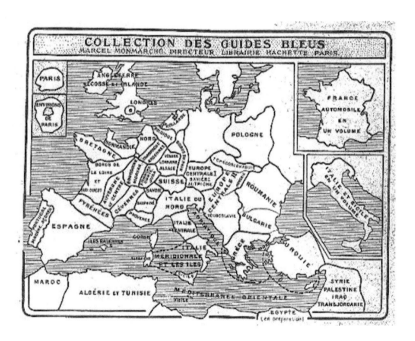

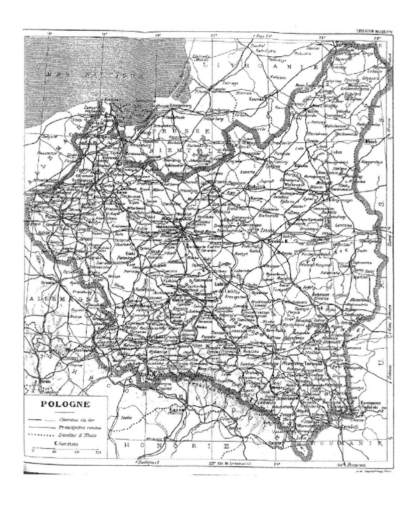